Exercise Technique Manual for Resistance Training

THIRD EDITION

National Strength and Conditioning Association

HUMAN KINETICS

Library of Congress Cataloging-in-Publication Data

Exercise technique manual for resistance training / National Strength and Conditioning Association. -- Third edition.

 pages cm

1. Weight training. 2. Free weights. 3. Exercise. 4. Personal trainers. I. National Strength & Conditioning Association (U.S.). Certification Commission.

 GV546.E96 2016

 613.7'1--dc23

2015016764

ISBN: 978-1-4925-0692-8 (print)

The web addresses cited in this text were current as of October 2015, unless otherwise noted.

Acquisitions Editor: Roger W. Earle; **Senior Developmental Editor:** Christine M. Drews; **Managing Editor:** Karla Walsh; **Copyeditor:** Ann Prisland; **Senior Graphic Designer:** Keri Evans; **Cover Designer:** Keith Blomberg; **Photograph (cover):** Neil Bernstein, © Human Kinetics; **Photographs (interior):** Neil Bernstein, © Human Kinetics; **Visual Production Assistant:** Joyce Brumfield; **Photo Production Manager:** Jason Allen; **Printer:** Walsworth

This book was edited by Matthew Sandstead, BA, NSCA-CPT,*D; Scott Caulfield, BS, CSCS,*D, RSCC*D; and Douglas Berninger, MEd, CSCS,*D, RSCC. The editors thank The Fitness Center in Champaign, Illinois, and the National Strength and Conditioning Association in Colorado Springs, Colorado, for assistance in providing the locations for the photo shoot for this book.

The video contents of this product are licensed for educational public performance for viewing by a traditional (live) audience, via closed circuit television, or via computerized local area networks within a single building or geographically unified campus. To request a license to broadcast these contents to a wider audience—for example, throughout a school district or state, or on a television station—please contact your sales representative **(www.HumanKinetics.com/SalesRepresentatives)**.

Printed in the United States of America   10 9 8 7 6

The paper in this book was manufactured using responsible forestry methods.

Human Kinetics
1607 N. Market St.
Champaign, IL 61820
Website: www.HumanKinetics.com

In the United States, email info@hkusa.com or call 800-747-4457.
In Canada, email info@hkcanada.com.
In the United Kingdom/Europe, email hk@hkeurope.com.

For information about Human Kinetics' coverage in other areas of the world, please visit our website: **www.HumanKinetics.com**

E6493

Tell us what you think!
Human Kinetics would love to hear what we can do to improve the customer experience. Use this QR code to take our brief survey.

Contents

Preface

The National Strength and Conditioning Association (NSCA) developed this manual primarily for those preparing for the Certified Strength and Conditioning Specialist (CSCS), NSCA-Certified Personal Trainer (NSCA-CPT), Certified Special Population Specialist (CSPS), and Tactical Strength and Conditioning Facilitator (TSAC-F) certification exams. When used in conjunction with the online video clips, exam candidates will become especially prepared for questions relating to anatomy, biomechanics, program design (e.g., exercise selection), and exercise technique.

Exercise Technique Manual for Resistance Training, Third Edition, also serves as an excellent resource for strength and conditioning professionals, health and fitness instructors, and personal trainers using resistance training exercises in their own programs or when instructing others. College and university faculty and students will find that this manual and the online video clips complement hands-on instruction and aid in teaching exercise technique without requiring the use of a weight room.

eBook available at your campus bookstore or HumanKinetics.com

This manual describes proper technique for 54 free weight and 16 machine exercises. The exercise technique checklists identify the primary muscle groups involved and the correct grip, stance, body position, and range of motion for each exercise. Additionally, descriptions of joint actions, spotting suggestions, and tips for avoiding injury are provided.

Although the exercise technique checklists were written by experts, no one should attempt to perform a new exercise without the supervision of a certified professional. It is also recommended that anyone considering participating in an exercise program consult a physician before beginning the program.

For more information on other certification exam preparation materials, please contact the NSCA at 719-632-6722 (or toll-free at 800-815-6826) or visit www.nsca.com.

Accessing the Online Video

New to this edition is high-definition online streaming video. The video clips demonstrate correct and incorrect technique for every exercise in the book. The online video can be accessed by visiting www.HumanKinetics.com/ ExerciseTechniqueManualForResistanceTraining. If you purchased a new print book, follow the directions included on the orange-framed page at the front of your book. That page includes access steps and the unique key code that you'll need the first time you visit the *Exercise Technique Manual for Resistance Training* website. If you purchased an e-book from HumanKinetics.com, follow the access instructions that were e-mailed to you after your purchase.

Once at the *Exercise Technique Manual for Resistance Training* website, select Online Video in the ancillary items box. You'll then see an Online Video page. Follow the links to the exercise you want to view. Once you select an exercise, you'll see a video player. The video numbers along the right side of the player correspond with video number cross-references in the book, and the title under the player corresponds with the exercise title in the book. Scroll through the list of clips until you find the video you want to watch. Select that clip, and the full video will play.

Introduction

This manual describes proper technique for 54 free weight and 16 machine exercises that are categorized into the following groups:

- Power and explosive (total body)
- Hip and thigh (multijoint and single joint)
- Calf (single joint)
- Chest (multijoint and single joint)
- Back (multijoint)
- Shoulder (multijoint and single joint)
- Biceps (single joint)
- Triceps (single joint)
- Forearm (single joint)
- Core
- Alternative modes and nontraditional implements

All exercises are illustrated in the online video, which can be accessed at www.HumanKinetics.com/ExerciseTechniqueManualForResistance Training.

Multijoint exercises involve two or more joints that change angles during the execution of a repetition (e.g., for the lower body during the power clean, this includes the hip, knee, and ankle joints). Single-joint exercises allow movement in only one joint during a repetition (e.g., the elbow joint during the biceps curl exercise). For the purposes of this manual, the joints of the shoulder girdle are combined with the true (glenohumeral) shoulder joint and, therefore, treated as one joint. For example, the lateral shoulder raise exercise is classified as a single-joint movement, despite the obvious involvement of several shoulder girdle joints in addition to the glenohumeral joint. Additionally, only the predominant muscles are included. Although many other muscles may assist during the exercise or may function as stabilizers, they are not included in the muscular involvement charts.

Each exercise description in this manual includes details about the following:

- Type of exercise
- Description of the action of movement
- Muscle group or body area trained
- Predominant muscle groups and muscles involved
- Guidelines for proper exercise technique listed in the order that they are performed
- Whether the exercise requires a spotter, as designated by the symbol shown here:

Spotting Guidelines

There are certain situations that warrant a spotter being present as an exercise is performed. The exercises that meet this requirement are categorized based on the location of the bar or dumbbells in relation to the lifter's body. Exercises that involve movement over the head or over the face need to be spotted to protect the lifter in case the bar or dumbbell falls on the lifter's head, neck, face, or torso and to help unrack and rack the bar in its supports, when needed. A spotter is also needed when a bar is placed on the back of a lifter's neck, across the shoulders, or on top of the anterior deltoids or clavicles.

Spotting Overhead Exercises and Those With the Bar on the Back or Front of the Shoulders

To promote safety, overhead exercises and those with the bar on the back or front of the shoulders should be performed inside a power rack with the crossbars set at an appropriate height based on the type of exercise and height of the lifter. The spotter (or spotters) needs to be as tall as the lifter and strong enough to be able to support the load, if necessary. Out-of-the-rack exercises (e.g., forward step lunge or step-up) with heavy weights can result in serious injury and should be spotted. Exercises in these situations include the following:

- Any variation of the shoulder press
- Any variation of the barbell squat
- Any variation of the barbell lunge

Spotting Over-the-Face Exercises

The spotter should grasp the bar with an alternated grip, usually narrower than the lifter's grip, when preparing for over-the-face exercises. The curved trajectory of the bar in some exercises (e.g., lying triceps extension) causes the spotter to have to use an alternated grip to pick up the bar and return it to the floor; however, a supinated grip should be used to spot the bar during execution of the exercise. Doing so helps ensure that the bar does not roll out of the spotter's hands and onto the lifter's face or neck. The spotter needs to establish a solid, wide base of support with the feet and maintain a neutral spine position to support the load that may have to be lifted in assistance of the lifter. Exercises in these situations include the following:

- Any variation of the bench press
- Lying barbell triceps extension
- Any variation of the dumbbell fly

General Safety Suggestions

Follow these guidelines to ensure safe exercise technique:

- Perform power and explosive exercises in a clean, dry, flat, well-marked area (e.g., on a lifting platform) free of obstacles and people.

This guideline can also apply to other complex nonpower exercises such as the lunge, deadlift, and step-up.

▶ If a repetition in a power or explosive exercise cannot be completed, push forward on the bar to move the body backward and let the bar fall to the floor. **Do not attempt to save a missed or failed repetition of this type of exercise.**

▶ Before performing exercises that finish with the bar overhead, check to see if there is sufficient floor-to-ceiling space.

▶ Use a bar with revolving sleeves, especially for the power and explosive exercises.

▶ Use a squat or power rack with the supporting pins or hooks set to position the bar at armpit height for the front squat and back squat; using that setting when beginning or ending an exercise with the bar at shoulder height is preferred to beginning or ending with the bar on the floor.

▶ When lifting the bar up and out of the supporting pins or hooks of a squat or power rack in preparation for an exercise, always step *backward* at the *beginning* of the set and step *forward* at the *end* of the set. **Do not walk backward to return the bar to the rack.**

▶ Always use collars and locks to secure free weight plates on the bar.

▶ Fully insert the selectorized pin or key (usually L or T shaped) into the weight stack for machine exercises.

Preparatory Body Position and Lifting Guidelines

A lifter often needs to lift a bar or dumbbells off the floor before getting into the starting position of an exercise (e.g., bent-over row, biceps curl, flat or incline dumbbell bench press or fly, upright row, lying barbell triceps extension, stiff-leg deadlift). To avoid excessive strain on the low back, place the body in the correct position to lift the weight safely and effectively.

First, use the correct stance in relation to the bar or dumbbells *and* properly grasp the bar or dumbbell handles:

▶ Squat down behind the bar or between the dumbbells.

▶ Place the feet between hip- and shoulder-width apart.

▶ If lifting a bar, position the bar close to the shins and over the balls of the feet and grasp the bar with a closed grip that is shoulder-width (or slightly wider) apart.

▶ If lifting dumbbells, stand directly between them and grasp the handles with a closed grip and a neutral arm or hand position.

▶ Position the arms outside the knees with the elbows extended.

Follow these six guidelines to place the body in the correct preparatory position *before* lifting a weight off the floor. These guidelines also describe how the body should be positioned immediately before the first repetition of a power exercise (e.g., power snatch, power clean):

1. The back is neutral or slightly arched.
2. The trapezius is relaxed and slightly stretched, the chest is held up and out, and the shoulder blades are held together.

3. The head is in line with the spine or slightly hyperextended.
4. The body's weight is balanced between the middle and balls of the feet, but the heels are in contact with the floor.
5. The shoulders are over or slightly in front of the bar.
6. The eyes are focused straight ahead or slightly upward.

To avoid frequent repetition, the checklists for many of the exercises in this manual refer to this six-item list of instructions as "preparatory body position and lifting guidelines." The full list is not provided for each exercise.

Weight Belt Recommendations

The use of a weight belt may help maintain intra-abdominal pressure while lifting. The appropriateness of a weight belt depends on the type of exercise performed and the relative load lifted. It is recommended that a weight belt be worn for exercises that place stress on the low back and during sets that use near-maximal or maximal loads. This strategy may help reduce the risk of injury to the low back when combined with proper lifting and spotting techniques. A shortcoming to weight belt use is that wearing a belt too often may reduce opportunities for the abdominal muscles to be trained. Furthermore, no weight belt is needed for exercises that do not stress the low back (e.g., biceps curl, lat pulldown) or for exercises that do stress the low back but involve the use of light loads (e.g., back squat, deadlift).

Breathing Guidelines

The best general guideline about proper breathing during a resistance training exercise is to exhale through the sticking point (the most difficult part of the exercise) of the concentric (exertion) phase and inhale during the easier part of the exercise (eccentric phase). Typically, the sticking point occurs soon after the transition from the eccentric phase to the concentric phase. For example, the sticking point of the free weight bench press exercise occurs about halfway through the upward movement phase. At that point, the lifter should exhale through this portion of the movement. As the bar is lowered back down to the chest, the lifter should inhale. This breathing strategy applies to nearly all resistance training exercises.

However, there are some situations in which breath holding may be suggested. For experienced and well-trained lifters performing **structural exercises** (those that load the vertebral column and therefore place stress on it) with high loads, the **Valsalva maneuver** can be helpful for maintaining proper vertebral alignment and support by increasing intra-abdominal pressure. The Valsalva maneuver involves expiring against a closed glottis, which, when combined with contracting the abdomen and rib cage muscles, creates rigid compartments of fluid in the lower torso and air in the upper torso (i.e., the fluid ball) and increases pressure within the abdomen.

The advantage of the Valsalva maneuver is that it increases the rigidity of the entire torso to aid in supporting the vertebral column, which in turn reduces the associated compressive forces on the disks during lifting. It also helps to establish and maintain a normal lordotic lumbar spine position (also called a *neutral spine*) and erect upper torso position described in the technique checklists for certain exercises. Be aware, however, that the resulting increase in intra-abdominal pressure has potentially detrimental side effects, such as dizziness, disorientation, excessively high blood pressure, and blackouts. This is why the breath-holding phase is—and should be—transient, only about 1 to 2 seconds (at most). Even a well-trained lifter should not extend the length of the breath-holding phase, because blood pressure can quickly rise to triple resting levels.

Strength and conditioning professionals involved in conducting 1-repetition maximum (1RM) tests in, for example, the power clean, power snatch, squat, deadlift, or bench press, need to be aware of the advantages and disadvantages of coaching lifters in the Valsalva maneuver. Although it is obviously important that the vertebral column be internally supported during these movements for safety and technique reasons, it is recommended that a lifter not extend the breath-holding period.

Exercises Using Alternative Modes and Nontraditional Implements

Exercises that involve alternative modes and nontraditional implements have become more common. The general guidelines employed in these types of exercises are similar to those used with traditional resistance training methods. Several guidelines should be followed when performing alternative or nontraditional implement exercises, including maintaining a stable body position, utilizing an appropriate grip, and following proper breathing patterns. The following are types of exercises that are not traditional to most training environments:

- Bodyweight exercises—Involve the use of the body's own weight as a form of external resistance through various movements
- Core stability and balance training methods—Include isolation exercises, the intentional use of machines or free weights, and instability devices to activate the core and improve balance
- Variable resistance—Allows the applied resistance to be varied in conjunction with changes in joint angle to maximize muscular force application throughout the full range of motion
- Nontraditional implements—Incorporates strongman exercises and kettlebell training to add greater variation to lifters' overall training
- Unilateral training—Integrated into a training program to reduce bilateral asymmetries or as a rehabilitation tool

TOTAL BODY

PART I

Power and Explosive Exercises

Name	Description of the concentric action	PREDOMINANT MUSCLES INVOLVED	
		Muscle group or body area	Muscles
Power snatch	Hip extension	Gluteals	Gluteus maximus
		Hamstrings	Semimembranosus
			Semitendinosus
			Biceps femoris
	Knee extension	Quadriceps	Vastus lateralis
			Vastus intermedius
			Vastus medialis
			Rectus femoris
	Ankle plantar flexion	Calf	Soleus
			Gastrocnemius
	Shoulder flexion and abduction	Shoulders	Anterior and medial deltoids
	Scapular elevation	Shoulder and upper back	Trapezius (upper portion)
	Elbow flexion	Upper arm (anterior)	Brachialis
			Biceps brachii
			Brachioradialis
	Elbow extension	Upper arm (posterior)	Triceps brachii
Hang power snatch	Same as the power snatch		
One-arm dumbbell snatch	Same as the power snatch		
Muscle snatch	Same as the power snatch		
Power clean	Same as the power snatch, but the concentric action does not include elbow extension		
Hang power clean	Same as the power snatch, but the concentric action does not include elbow extension		
Dumbbell hang power clean	Same as the power snatch, but the concentric action does not include elbow extension		
Push press	Same as the power snatch except there is greater shoulder flexion and abduction (anterior and medial deltoid) and greater triceps extension (triceps brachii)		
Push jerk	Same as the power snatch		
Split jerk	Same as the power snatch		

1.1 POWER SNATCH

Video 1.1

From the starting position, this exercise involves lifting the bar overhead with the arms fully extended—all in one movement. Although the upward movement consists of four distinct phases, the upward movement of the bar occurs in one *continuous* motion.

Starting Position

▸ Stand with the feet placed between hip- and shoulder-width apart with the toes pointed slightly outward so the knees track directly over the feet.

▸ Squat down with the hips lower than the shoulders and grasp the bar evenly with a pronated grip. The hand placement on the bar is wider than it is for other exercises. It can be estimated by measuring the distance from the knuckles' edge of a clenched fist of an arm extended out to the side and parallel to the floor, across the back of the arm and upper back, to the outside edge of the opposite shoulder. Alternatively, the lifter's grip width can be estimated by measuring the elbow-to-elbow distance when the upper arms are abducted directly out from the sides and parallel to

Grip measurement: fist-to-opposite-shoulder method

Grip measurement: elbow-to-elbow method

Starting position/
beginning of first pull

End of first pull/
beginning of transition

End of transition/
beginning of second pull

the floor. This distance is the space between the hands when they are grasping the bar. If necessary, this spacing can be modified depending on shoulder flexibility and arm length. The actual grip can be a closed grip or a hook grip. To use a hook grip, place a pronated hand on the bar and first wrap the thumb around the bar, then wrap the four fingers. The first one or two fingers, depending on their length, will cover the thumb. This grip is effective for lifting maximal or near-maximal loads, but it can be uncomfortable initially. Wrapping the thumbs with athletic tape will alleviate the pressure when using the hook grip.

- Position the arms outside the knees with the elbows fully extended and pointed out to the sides.

- Position the bar approximately 1 inch (3 cm) in front of the shins and over the balls of the feet.

- Just before liftoff, observe the preparatory body position and lifting guidelines to place the body in the correct position to lift the bar off the floor. All repetitions begin from this position.

- Exact positions of the torso, hips, knees, and bar are dependent on a lifter's joint segment lengths and lower body joint flexibility. An inflexible person attempting to get into the correct starting position of the power snatch may have difficulty grasping the bar with the elbows extended while keeping the heels on the floor. If the preparatory body position cannot be achieved, the hang power snatch is an alternative because it does not require the lifter to start with the bar on the floor. It instead begins with the bar above the knees.

End of second pull   Catch   End position

First Pull

The portion of the upward movement phase from liftoff to where the bar is just above the knees is termed the *first pull*.

- Begin the exercise by forcefully extending the hips and knees. These joints must extend at the same rate to keep the torso angle constant in relation to the floor. Do not let the hips rise before or faster than the shoulders. Maintaining the neutral (or slightly arched) spine position while shifting balance slowly from over the middle of the feet toward the heels helps in maintaining a constant torso angle.

- The elbows should still be fully extended, the head neutral in relation to the spine, and the shoulders over or slightly ahead of the bar.

- As the bar is raised, it should be kept as close to the shins as possible; slightly shifting the body's weight back toward the heels as the bar is lifted will promote proper bar trajectory.

Transition

The upward movement phase where the knees and thighs move forward under the bar is called the *transition*.

- As the bar rises to just above the knees, thrust the hips forward and slightly flex the knees to move the thighs against, and the knees under, the bar.

- During this second knee bend, the body's weight shifts forward toward the middle of the feet, but the heels remain in contact with the floor.

- Keep the back neutral or slightly arched, the elbows fully extended and pointed out to the sides, and the head in line with the spine.

- The shoulders should still be over the bar, although they will tend to move backward as the knees and thighs move under the bar. The body is in the power position at the end of this phase.

Second Pull (Power Phase)

The upward movement from the power position with the bar at the thighs and close to the body to where the lower body joints are fully extended and the bar has reached its maximum velocity is referred to as the *second pull* or *power phase*.

- The bar should be near to or in contact with the front of the thighs near the inguinal fold. Initiate a fast upward motion by quickly extending the hips, knees, and ankles. Note that ankle extension here refers to plantar flexion.

- The bar should pass as close to the body as possible.

- Maintain a torso position with the back neutral or slightly arched, the elbows pointing out to the sides, and the head in line with the spine.

- Keep the shoulders over the bar and the elbows extended as long as possible while the hips, knees, and ankles are extending.

- As the lower body joints fully extend, rapidly shrug the shoulders. The elbows should be extended and pointed out to the sides during the shrugging movement.

- As the shoulders reach their highest elevation, flex the elbows to begin pulling the body under the bar. The upper body movements are similar to the pright row exercise, only with a wider grip. The elbows move up and out to the sides.

- Continue to pull with the arms as high and as long as possible.

- Because of the triple extension of the lower body and the pulling effort of the upper body, the torso will be erect or slightly hyperextended, the head will be tilted slightly back, and the feet may lose contact with the floor.

Catch

The act of receiving the bar in the overhead position is called the *catch*.

- After the lower body has fully extended and the bar reaches near-maximal height, pull the body under the bar by rotating the arms and hands around and then under the bar and by flexing the hips and knees to approximately a quarter-squat position.

- The feet typically regain contact with the floor in a slightly wider stance with the toes pointed out slightly farther than at the starting position.

- Once the arms are under the bar, extend the elbows quickly to push the bar upward and the body downward under the bar.

- The bar should be caught over and slightly behind the ears with

  - fully extended elbows,
  - an erect and stable torso,
  - a neutral head position,
  - flat feet, and
  - the body's weight over the middle of the feet.

- The quarter-squat position should be reached with the elbows fully extended just as the bar reaches its maximum height.

- After gaining control and balance, stand up by extending the hips and knees to a fully erect position.

Downward Movement

- If bumper plates are used, the bar can be returned to the floor with a controlled drop; the bounce of the plates should be controlled with the hands on or near the bar.

- Most commonly, the bar is lowered slowly from the overhead position by gradually reducing the muscular tension of the shoulders to allow a controlled descent of the bar to the thighs. The hips and knees are simultaneously flexed to cushion the impact of the bar on the thighs. The bar is then lowered by squatting down until it touches the floor.

- Reposition the bar and the body for the next repetition, if applicable.

1.2   HANG POWER SNATCH

Video 1.2

This exercise is similar to the power snatch with one primary modification—the initial position of the bar is on the thighs, just above the knees, not on the floor. Fundamentally, the hang power snatch *is* the power snatch exercise starting at the beginning of the transition. Because the bar is moved a shorter distance, there is less time for the lifter to exert a pulling force on the bar. Since there is no initial momentum of the bar at the knees, more muscular effort (power) is required for lifting a given load than in the power snatch. Therefore, the forceful, rapid extension of the hips, knees, and ankles followed by the shrugging of the shoulders and pulling with the arms is critical for performing the hang power snatch exercise.

Starting Position

▶ Stand with the feet placed between hip- and shoulder-width apart with the toes pointed slightly outward so the knees track directly over the feet.

▶ Squat down with the hips lower than the shoulders and grasp the bar evenly with a pronated grip. The hand placement on the bar is wider than it is for other exercises. It can be estimated by measuring the distance from the knuckles' edge of a clenched fist of an arm extended out to the side and parallel to the floor, across the back of

Starting position   Downward movement   Upward movement

the arm and upper back, to the outside edge of the opposite shoulder. Alternatively, the lifter's grip width can be estimated by measuring the elbow-to-elbow distance when the upper arms are abducted directly out from the sides and parallel to the floor. This distance is the space between the hands when they are grasping the bar. If necessary, this spacing can be modified depending on shoulder flexibility and arm length. The actual grip can be a closed grip or a hook grip. To use a hook grip, place a pronated hand on the bar and first wrap the thumb around the bar, then wrap the four fingers. The first one or two fingers, depending on their length, will cover the thumb. This grip is effective for lifting maximal or near-maximal loads, but it can be uncomfortable initially. Wrapping the thumbs with athletic tape will alleviate the pressure when using the hook grip.

- Position the arms outside the knees with the elbows fully extended and pointed out to the sides.
- Lift the bar off the floor and stand erect, so that the bar is near the inguinal fold of the hips. All repetitions begin from this position.

Downward Movement

This movement is initiated by a descent (eccentric contraction of the hamstrings), where the lifter lowers the bar to the midthigh, top of the knee, or below the knee. Balance is shifted from the middle of the foot to closer to the heel as the bar is lowered.

Catch   Standing tall

Transition

The portion of the upward movement where the knees and thighs move forward under the bar is called the *transition*.

- Once the bar reaches the lowest position of the downward movement, the lifter quickly reverses the action by utilizing the stretch-shortening cycle of the hamstrings to begin to accelerate the bar upward.

- The hips move forward as the knees slightly flex to move the thighs against, and the knees under, the bar.

- As the knees flex, the body's weight shifts forward toward the middle of the feet, but the heels remain in contact with the floor.

- Keep the back neutral (or slightly arched), the elbows fully extended and pointed out to the sides, and the head in line with the spine.

- The shoulders should still be over the bar, although they will tend to move backward as the knees and thighs move under the bar. The body is in the power position at the end of this phase.

Upward Movement (Power Phase)

The upward movement from the power position with the bar at the thighs and close to the body to where the lower body joints are fully extended and the bar has reached its maximum velocity is referred to as the *power phase*.

- The bar should be near to or in contact with the front of the thighs, close to the inguinal fold. Initiate a fast, upward motion by quickly extending the hips, knees, and ankles. Note that ankle extension here refers to plantar flexion.

- The bar should pass as close to the body as possible.

- Maintain a torso position with the back neutral or slightly arched, the elbows pointed out to the sides, and the head in line with the spine.

- Keep the shoulders over the bar and the elbows extended as long as possible while the hips, knees, and ankles are extending.

- As the lower body joints fully extend, rapidly shrug the shoulders. The elbows should be extended and pointed out to the sides during the shrugging movement.

- As the shoulders reach their highest elevation, flex the elbows to begin pulling the body under the bar with the arms. The upper body movements are similar to the upright row exercise, only with a wider grip. The elbows move up and out to the sides, but not backward.

- Because of the triple extension of the lower body and the pulling effort of the upper body, the torso will be erect or slightly hyperextended, the head will be tilted slightly back, and the feet may lose contact with the floor.

Catch

The act of receiving the bar in the overhead position is called the *catch*.

- After the lower body has fully extended and the bar reaches near-maximal height, pull the body under the bar by quickly rotating the elbows around, and then under, the bar.
- Once the elbows are under the bar, fully extend the elbows quickly to push the bar upward and the body downward under the bar.
- The hips and knees simultaneously flex into approximately a quarter-squat position.
- The feet typically regain contact with the floor by quickly moving into a slightly wider stance with the toes pointed out slightly farther than at the starting position.
- The bar should be caught over and slightly behind the ears with
  - fully extended elbows,
  - an erect and tight torso,
  - a neutral head position,
  - flat feet, and
  - the body's weight over the middle of the feet.
- Ideally, the quarter-squat position will be reached with the elbows extended just as the bar reaches its maximum height.
- After gaining control and balance, stand up by extending the hips and knees to a fully erect position.

Downward Movement

- Most commonly, the bar is lowered slowly from the overhead position by gradually reducing the muscular tension of the shoulders to allow a controlled descent of the bar to the thighs. The hips and knees are simultaneously flexed to cushion the impact of the bar on the thighs.
- Reposition the bar and the body for the next repetition, if applicable.

TOTAL BODY

1.3   ONE-ARM DUMBBELL SNATCH

Video 1.3

Starting Position

▸ Straddle a dumbbell on the floor and place the feet between hip- and shoulder-width apart with the toes pointed slightly outward.

▸ Squat down with the hips lower than the shoulders and grasp the dumbbell with a closed, pronated grip with the elbow fully extended.

▸ The arm that is not holding the dumbbell should hang down next to that side of the body.

▸ Just before liftoff, observe the preparatory body position and lifting guidelines to place the body in the correct position to lift the dumbbell off the floor. All repetitions begin from this position.

Upward Movement

▸ Begin the exercise by forcefully extending the hips, knees, and ankles (commonly called the *triple extension*).

Starting position   Upward movement

▱ The dumbbell should slide up the thigh, or remain very close to the thigh, as it accelerates upward.

▱ The elbow of the arm holding the dumbbell should remain extended as the knees, hips, and ankles are extending.

▱ As the lower body joints fully extend, rapidly shrug the shoulder of the arm holding the dumbbell. The elbow of the arm holding the dumbbell should be extended and pointed out to the side during the shrugging movement.

▱ As the shoulder reaches its highest elevation, flex the elbow holding the dumbbell to begin pulling the body under the dumbbell. The dumbbell should pass as close to the torso as possible.

▱ Continue to pull with the arm holding the dumbbell as high and as long as possible.

▱ The arm that is not holding the dumbbell should remain on the opposite hip or be held to the side.

▱ Because of the triple extension of the lower body and the pulling effort of the upper body, the torso will be erect, the head will be tilted slightly back, and the feet may lose contact with the floor.

Catch   Standing position

Catch

▶ After the lower body has fully extended and the dumbbell reaches near-maximal height, pull the body under the dumbbell by rotating the arm and hand holding the dumbbell around and then under the dumbbell and by flexing the hips and knees to approximately a quarter-squat position.

▶ Once the arm holding the dumbbell is under the dumbbell, extend the elbow quickly to push the dumbbell up and the body downward under the dumbbell.

▶ The quarter-squat position should be reached with the elbow of the arm holding the dumbbell fully extended just as the dumbbell reaches its maximum height.

▶ The arm that is not holding the dumbbell should remain on the opposite hip or be held to the side.

▶ After gaining control and balance, stand up to a fully erect position.

Downward Movement

▶ At the completion of the repetition, slowly lower the dumbbell from the overhead position by gradually reducing the muscular tension of the shoulder of the arm holding the dumbbell; allow a controlled descent of the dumbbell first to the shoulder, then the thigh, and finally to the floor between the feet, using a squatting movement.

▶ Reposition the dumbbell and the body for the next repetition, if applicable.

1.4 MUSCLE SNATCH

Video 1.4

From the starting position, the muscle snatch exercise involves lifting the bar overhead with the arms fully extended. This is slightly different from the power snatch, which is one continuous movement. The muscle snatch is divided into two movements: The elbows rotate under the bar and then the bar is pressed out to finish the movement. The hips and knees do not flex to receive the bar in the muscle snatch.

Starting Position

- Stand with the feet placed between hip- and shoulder-width apart with the toes pointed slightly outward so the knees track directly over the feet.

- Squat down with the hips lower than the shoulders and grasp the bar evenly with a pronated grip. The hand placement on the bar is wider than it is for other exercises. It can be estimated by measuring the distance from the knuckles' edge of a clenched fist of an arm extended out to the side and parallel to the floor, across the back of the arm and upper back, to the outside edge of the opposite shoulder. Alternatively, the lifter's grip width can be estimated by measuring the elbow-to-elbow distance when the upper arms are abducted directly out from the sides and parallel to the floor. This distance is the space between the hands when they are grasping the bar. If necessary, this spacing can be modified depending on shoulder flexibility and arm length. The actual grip can be a closed grip or a hook grip. To use a hook grip, place a pronated hand on the bar and first wrap the thumb around the bar, then wrap the four fingers. The first one or two fingers, depending on their length, will cover the thumb. This grip is effective for lifting maximal or near-maximal loads, but it can be uncomfortable initially. Wrapping the thumbs with athletic tape will alleviate the pressure when using the hook grip.

- Position the arms outside the knees with the elbows fully extended and pointed out to the sides.

- Position the bar approximately 1 inch (3 cm) in front of the shins and over the balls of the feet.

- Just before liftoff, observe the preparatory body position and lifting guidelines to place the body in the correct position to lift the bar off the floor. All repetitions begin from this position.

- Exact positions of the torso, hips, knees, and bar are dependent on a lifter's segment lengths and lower body joint flexibility. An inflexible person attempting to get into the correct starting position of the muscle snatch may have difficulty grasping the bar with the elbows extended while keeping the heels on the floor. If the preparatory body position cannot be achieved, the lifter can perform the exercise from the hang starting position as an alternative because it does not require the lifter to start with the bar on the floor. It instead begins with the bar above the knees.

First Pull

The portion of the upward movement phase from liftoff to where the bar is just above the knees is termed the *first pull*.

- Begin the exercise by forcefully extending the hips and knees. These joints must extend at the same rate to keep the torso angle constant in relation to the floor. Do not let the hips rise before or faster than the shoulders. Maintaining the neutral (or slightly arched) back position while shifting balance slowly from over the middle of the feet toward the heels helps in maintaining a constant torso angle.
- The elbows should still be fully extended, the head in line with the spine, and the shoulders over or slightly ahead of the bar.
- As the bar is raised, it should be kept as close to the shins as possible; slightly shifting the body's weight back toward the heels as the bar is lifted will promote proper bar trajectory.

Transition

The portion of the upward movement where the knees and thighs move forward under the bar is called the *transition*.

MUSCLE SNATCH

| Starting position | First pull | Transition |

- As the bar rises to just above the knees, thrust the hips forward and slightly flex the knees to move the thighs against, and the knees under, the bar.

- During this second knee bend, the body's weight shifts forward toward the middle of the feet, but the heels remain in contact with the floor.

- Keep the back neutral or slightly arched, the elbows fully extended and pointed out to the sides, and the head in line with the spine.

- Keep the shoulders over the bar, although they will tend to move backward as the knees and thighs move under the bar. The body is in the power position at the end of this phase.

Second Pull (Power Phase)

The upward movement from the power position with the bar at the thighs and close to the body to where the lower body joints are fully extended and the bar has reached its maximum velocity is referred to as the *second pull* or *power phase*.

- The bar should be near to or in contact with the front of the thighs above the knees. Initiate a fast upward motion by quickly extending the hips, knees, and ankles. Note that ankle extension here refers to plantar flexion.

Second pull   Catch   Finish

▶ The bar should pass as close to the body as possible.

▶ Maintain a torso position with the back neutral or slightly arched, the elbows pointed out to the sides, and the head in line with the spine.

▶ Keep the shoulders over the bar and the elbows extended as long as possible while the hips, knees, and ankles are extending.

▶ As the lower body joints fully extend, rapidly shrug the shoulders. The elbows should be extended and pointed out to the sides during the shrugging movement.

▶ As the shoulders reach their highest elevation, flex the elbows to begin pulling the bar up. The upper body movements are similar to the upright row exercise, only with a wider grip. The elbows move up and out to the sides.

▶ After the lower body has fully extended and the elbows reach their highest point, they are rotated under the bar quickly so that they point toward the floor. Upon full extension, the knees and hips remain extended to finish the movement. They do not flex to receive the bar as is done in the power snatch.

Catch

The act of pressing the bar in the overhead position is also called the *receiving phase* of the muscle snatch.

▶ Once the elbows are directly underneath the bar, press the bar overhead.

▶ Unlike in the power snatch, the knees and hips are fully extended and do not flex as the bar is pressed overhead.

Downward Movement

▶ If bumper plates are used, the bar can be returned to the floor with a controlled drop; the bounce of the plates should be controlled with the hands on or near the bar.

▶ Most commonly, the bar is lowered slowly from the overhead position by gradually reducing the muscular tension of the upper body to allow a controlled descent of the bar to the thighs. The hips and knees are simultaneously flexed to cushion the impact of the bar on the thighs. The bar is then lowered by squatting down until it touches the floor.

▶ Reposition the bar and the body for the next repetition, if applicable.

1.5 POWER CLEAN

Video 1.5

This exercise is similar to the power snatch but with two major differences:

1. The final bar position is at the shoulders, not over the head.
2. The grip is approximately shoulder-width apart, whereas the snatch has a considerably wider grip.

Because of the many commonalities, the description of the power clean technique is slightly abbreviated and emphasis is placed on the unique aspects of this exercise in comparison to the power snatch.

Starting Position

- Stand with the feet placed between hip- and shoulder-width apart with the toes pointed slightly outward so the knees track directly over the feet.
- Squat down with the hips lower than the shoulders and grasp the bar evenly with a shoulder-width (or slightly wider), pronated grip.
- Position the arms outside the knees with the elbows fully extended and pointed out to the sides.
- Position the bar approximately 1 inch (3 cm) in front of the shins and over the balls of the feet.
- Just before liftoff, observe the preparatory body position and lifting guidelines to place the body in the correct position to lift the bar off the floor. All repetitions begin from this position.
- Exact positions of the torso, hips, knees, and bar are related to the lifter's body segment length and lower body joint flexibility. An alternative exercise is the hang power clean, which begins with the bar just above the knees instead of on the floor.

First Pull

- Begin the exercise by forcefully extending the hips and knees. Keep the torso angle constant in relation to the floor, do not let the hips rise before or faster than the shoulders, and keep the back neutral or slightly arched.
- Maintain full elbow extension, with the head in line with the spine, and the shoulders over or slightly ahead of the bar.
- Keep the bar as close to the shins as possible.

Transition

- As the bar rises to just above the knees, thrust the hips forward and slightly flex the knees to move the thighs against, and the knees under, the bar.

- As the knees flex, shift the body's weight forward toward the middle of the feet, keeping the heels on the floor.
- Maintain a neutral or slightly arched back, with the elbows fully extended and pointed out to the sides, the shoulders over or slightly ahead of the bar, and the head in line with the spine.
- At the finish of the transition, the body is in position for the second pull (power phase).

Second Pull (Power Phase)

- From this position with the bar on the thighs between the knees and middle of the thighs, start the second pull by forcefully and quickly extending the hips, knees, and ankles.
- The bar should pass as close to the torso as possible.
- Keep the shoulders over the bar and the elbows extended as long as possible while the hips, knees, and ankles are extending.
- As the lower body joints fully extend, rapidly shrug the shoulders. The elbows should be kept extended and pointed out to the sides during the shrugging movement.

POWER CLEAN

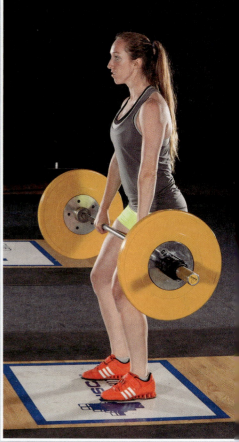

Starting position/
beginning of first pull

End of first pull/
beginning of transition

End of transition/
beginning of second pull

- As the shoulders reach their highest elevation, flex the elbows to begin pulling the body under the bar.
- Continue to pull with the arms as high and as long as possible with the elbows moving up and out to the sides.
- The upward momentum from the triple extension will result in an erect or slightly hyperextended torso and head, and the feet may come off the floor.

Catch

The catch phase of the power clean ends with the bar on the anterior deltoids and clavicles, similar to the arm and bar position of the front squat exercise.

- As the second pull ends with the bar at maximal height, pull the body under the bar by rotating the arms and hands around and then under the bar and by flexing the hips and knees to approximately a quarter-squat position.
- The feet will regain contact with the floor in a slightly wider stance in comparison to the starting position.

End of second pull   Catch   End position

▶ The bar should be caught at the anterior deltoids and clavicles with the

- head facing forward,
- neck neutral or slightly hyperextended,
- wrists hyperextended,
- elbows fully flexed,
- upper arms parallel to the floor,
- back neutral or slightly arched,
- feet flat on the floor, and
- body's weight over the middle of the feet.

▶ The bar should be caught with the torso almost fully erect and the shoulders slightly ahead of the buttocks. This position, which parallels the body position during the beginning of the downward movement of the front squat, allows the bar to be directly over the center of gravity.

▶ If the torso is too erect, the momentum of the bar will push the shoulders backward and hyperextend the low back, resulting in an increased risk of injury.

▶ After gaining control and balance, stand up to a fully erect position.

Downward Movement

▶ At the completion of the repetition, rotate the arms back around the bar to unrack it from the anterior deltoids and clavicles, and slowly lower the bar down to the thighs. Slightly flex the hips and knees to cushion the impact of the bar on the thighs.

▶ Slowly flex the hips and knees at the same rate (to keep an erect torso position) to return the bar to the floor in a controlled manner.

▶ Reposition the bar and the body for the next repetition.

1.6 HANG POWER CLEAN

Video 1.6

This exercise is similar to the power clean with one primary modification—the initial position of the bar is not on the floor. Fundamentally, the hang power clean *is* the power clean exercise starting at the beginning of the transition. Because the bar is moved a shorter distance, there is less time for the lifter to exert a pulling force on the bar. Since there is no initial momentum of the bar at the knees, more muscular effort (power) is required for lifting a given load than in the power clean. Therefore, the forceful, rapid extension of the hips, knees, and ankles followed by the shrugging of the shoulders and pulling with the arms is critical for performing the hang power clean exercise.

Starting Position

- Observe the preparatory body position and lifting guidelines to place the body in the correct position to lift the bar off the floor.

- Using the same stance, grip, and initial body position as the power clean, slowly lift the bar along the shins and thighs until standing erect with the bar resting on the front of the thighs.

- From this standing position with the arms extended and the elbows pointed out to the sides, lean forward and flex the hips and knees to place the bar just above the knees.

- All repetitions begin from this position.

Upward Movement

- Begin the exercise by forcefully extending the hips, knees, and ankles (commonly called the triple extension).

- Keep the shoulders over the bar and the elbows extended as long as possible. As the lower body joints fully extend, rapidly shrug the shoulders but keep the elbows extended and pointed out to the sides.

- At maximal shoulder elevation, flex the elbows and pull the body under the bar. The bar should pass as close to the torso as possible.

- Continue to pull with the arms as high and as long as possible. These actions will result in the highest bar position.

- This triple extension will result in an erect or slightly hyperextended torso and head, and the feet may come off the floor.

Catch

- After the lower body has fully extended and the bar reaches maximal height, pull the body under the bar by rotating the arms and hands around and then under the bar and by flexing the hips and knees to approximately a quarter-squat position.

TOTAL BODY

- Catch the bar at the anterior deltoids and clavicles with the elbows slightly forward of the bar.
- The feet will regain contact with the floor in a slightly wider stance in comparison to the starting position.
- After gaining control and balance, stand up to a fully erect position.

Downward Movement

- At the completion of the repetition, rotate the arms and hands back around the bar to unrack it from the anterior deltoids and clavicles, and slowly lower the bar down to the thighs. Slightly flex the hips and knees to cushion the impact of the bar on the thighs.

HANG POWER CLEAN

Starting position   Transition

- If additional repetitions are to be performed, stand fully erect first and then follow the guidelines to move the body into the correct starting position. The bar does not return to the floor between repetitions.

- At the completion of the set, slowly flex the hips and knees at the same rate (to keep an erect torso position) to return the bar to the floor in a controlled manner.

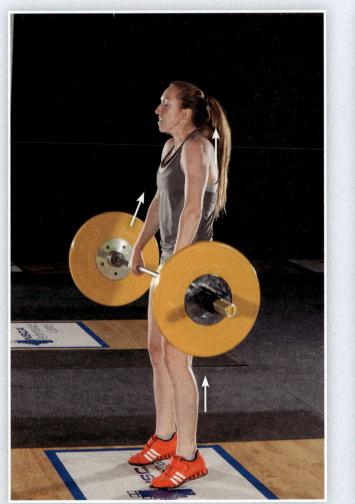

Triple extension with shoulder shrug

Catch

1.7   DUMBBELL HANG POWER CLEAN

Video 1.7

Starting Position

▸ Grasp two dumbbells with a closed grip.

▸ Observe the preparatory body position and lifting guidelines to place the body in the correct position to lift the dumbbells off the floor.

▸ Slowly lift the dumbbells along the shins and knees until standing erect with the dumbbells resting on the front of the thighs, or near the sides of the thighs.

▸ From this standing position with the arms fully extended, lean forward and flex the hips and knees to place the dumbbells slightly above or below the knees, depending on the length of the lifter's torso and arms.

▸ All repetitions begin from this position.

Starting position

Upward movement

Upward Movement

▸ Begin the exercise by forcefully extending the hips, knees, and ankles (commonly called the triple extension).

▸ The dumbbells should slide up the thighs, or remain very close to the thighs, as they accelerate upward.

▸ Keep the shoulders over the dumbbells and the elbows extended as long as possible. As the lower body joints fully extend, rapidly shrug the shoulders but keep the elbows extended and pointed out to the sides.

▸ At maximal shoulder elevation, flex the elbows. The dumbbells should pass as close to the torso as possible.

▸ Continue to pull with the arms as high and as long as possible.

▸ This triple extension will result in an erect or slightly hyperextended torso and head, and the feet may come off the floor.

Catch

Catch

▶ After the lower body has fully extended and the dumbbells reach maximal height, pull the body under the dumbbells by rotating the arms and hands around and then under the dumbbells and by flexing the hips and knees to approximately a quarter-squat position.

▶ Catch the dumbbells at the anterior deltoids and clavicles with the elbows slightly forward of the dumbbells.

▶ The feet will regain contact with the floor in a slightly wider stance in comparison to the starting position.

▶ After gaining control and balance, stand up to a fully erect position.

Downward Movement

▶ At the completion of the repetition, rotate the arms and hands back around the dumbbells to unrack them from the anterior deltoids and clavicles, and slowly lower the dumbbells down to the thighs. Slightly flex the hips and knees to cushion the impact of the dumbbells on the thighs.

▶ If additional repetitions are to be performed, stand fully erect first and then follow the guidelines to move the body into the correct starting position. Do not return the dumbbells to the floor between repetitions.

▶ At the completion of the set, slowly flex the hips and knees at the same rate (to keep an erect torso position) to return the dumbbells to the floor in a controlled manner.

1.8   PUSH PRESS

Video 1.8

This exercise consists of quickly and forcefully flexing and then extending the hips and knees to push the bar from the shoulders to over the head. Although the upward movement consists of two phases, the movement of the bar occurs in one continuous motion without interruption. The push press exercise involves a rapid hip and knee extension that accelerates the bar off the shoulders. The hip and knee extension thrust is only forceful enough to drive the bar one-half to two-thirds the distance overhead. From this height, the bar is pressed out (hence the name *push press*) to the overhead position, with the hips and knees remaining fully extended after the thrust.

Starting Position

- Use the power clean or hang power clean exercise to lift the bar from the floor to the shoulders, or remove the bar from a shoulder-height position on a power or squat rack.

- Stand erect with the feet hip- to shoulder-width apart and the toes pointed forward or slightly outward.

- Once the bar is positioned at the front of the shoulders, check to be sure that the grip on the bar is even, pronated, closed, and about shoulder-width apart. The grip should remain relaxed on the bar.

- The elbows should be underneath or slightly ahead of the bar.

- All repetitions begin from this position.

Dip (Active Preparation for the Drive Phase)

- While keeping the torso erect and head in a neutral position, flex the hips and knees at a slow to moderate speed to move the bar in a straight downward path. Do not change the position of the arms.

- The hips should not move backward during the dip. Instead, they should remain directly underneath the shoulders.

- This downward movement is not a full squat, but rather a dip to a depth not to exceed a quarter squat or the catch position of the power clean. Another guideline is a depth that does not exceed 10% of the lifter's body height.

Upward Movement (Drive Phase)

- Immediately upon reaching the lowest position of the dip, reverse the movement by rapidly extending the hips, knees, and ankles to move the bar overhead.

- Initially, the bar needs to be held in place on the shoulders to benefit maximally from the upward momentum produced by the triple extension. Note that the heels may come off the floor as the bar leaves the shoulders.

- The neck must slightly hyperextend to allow the bar to pass by the chin (or else the bar will hit the face).

Catch

The drive phase of the push press is not forceful enough to move the bar to an overhead position. Since the hips and knees are already fully extended after the drive, the shoulders (deltoids) and elbows (triceps) must extend to press the bar up to an overhead position.

▸ Once the bar is overhead, establish the following positions:

- Fully extended elbows
- Erect, stable torso
- Neutral head position
- Flat feet
- Bar over or slightly behind the ears

▸ Balance the body's weight over the middle of the feet.

▸ Stand in a fully erect body position to gain control of the bar and achieve balance.

PUSH PRESS

Starting position   Dip

Downward Movement

▸ At the completion of the repetition, lower the bar by gradually reducing the muscular tension of the arms to allow a controlled descent of the bar to the shoulders. The hips and knees are simultaneously flexed to cushion the impact of the bar on the shoulders.

▸ If additional repetitions are to be performed, stand fully erect first and then follow the guidelines described for the dip phase. Do not return the bar to the floor or rack between repetitions.

▸ At the completion of the set, first lower the bar from the shoulders to the thighs, then to the floor (similar to the power clean exercise). The bar can also be placed back on the power or squat rack.

Drive   Catch (push press)

1.9   PUSH JERK

This exercise consists of quickly and forcefully flexing and then extending the hips and knees to drive the bar upward from the shoulders while pushing the body underneath. The bar finishes in an overhead position. The push jerk exercise requires a rapid hip and knee extension to accelerate the bar off the shoulders. The push jerk also involves a forceful hip and knee thrust so that the bar is actually thrown (or *jerked*) upward, then caught with extended elbows in the overhead position with the hips and knees slightly flexed.

Starting Position

▶ Use the power clean or hang power clean exercise to lift the bar from the floor to the shoulders or remove the bar from a shoulder-height position on a power or squat rack.

▶ Stand erect with the feet hip- to shoulder-width apart and the toes pointed forward or slightly outward.

Starting position   Dip   Drive

- Once the bar is positioned at the front of the shoulders, check to be sure that the grip on the bar is even, pronated, closed, and slightly wider than shoulder-width. The grip should remain relaxed on the bar.
- The elbows should be underneath or slightly ahead of the bar.
- All repetitions begin from this position.

Dip (Active Preparation for the Drive Phase)

- While keeping the torso erect and head in line with the spine, flex the hips and knees at a slow to moderate speed to move the bar in a straight downward path. Do not change the position of the arms.
- The hips should not move backward during the dip. Instead, they should remain directly underneath the shoulders.
- The downward movement is not a full squat, but rather a dip to a depth not to exceed a quarter squat or the catch position of the power clean. Another guideline is a depth that does not exceed 10% of the lifter's body height.

Catch (push jerk)   Recovery position

Upward Movement (Drive Phase)

- Immediately upon reaching the lowest position of the dip, reverse the movement by rapidly extending the hips, knees, ankles, and then the elbows to move the bar overhead.

- Initially, the bar needs to be held in place on the shoulders to benefit maximally from the upward momentum produced by the triple extension. Note that the feet may come off the floor as the bar leaves the shoulders.

- The neck must slightly hyperextend to allow the bar to pass by the chin (or else the bar will hit the face).

Catch

The drive phase of the push jerk allows the bar to be caught over the head with the elbows fully extended and the hips and knees slightly flexed.

- As the bar is caught, the hips and knees should be flexed to about a quarter-squat position. The goal is to catch the bar at the same moment the bar reaches maximal height and the feet come back into contact with the floor.

- The torso should be erect, with the head in line with the spine directly under the bar; the eyes are focused forward.

- Balance the body's weight over the middle of the feet.

Recovery

- After gaining control and balance, stand up by extending the hips and knees to a fully erect position with the feet flat on the floor.

- Keep the elbows locked while the bar is stabilized overhead.

Downward Movement

- At the completion of the repetition, lower the bar by gradually reducing the muscular tension of the arms to allow a controlled descent of the bar to the shoulders. The hips and knees are simultaneously flexed to cushion the impact of the bar on the shoulders.

- If additional repetitions are to be performed, stand fully erect first and then follow the guidelines described for the dip phase. The bar does not return to the floor or rack between repetitions.

- At the completion of the set, first lower the bar from the shoulders to the thighs, then to the floor (similar to the power clean exercise). The bar can also be placed back on the power or squat rack.

1.10 SPLIT JERK

Video 1.10

This exercise consists of quickly and forcefully flexing and then extending the hips and knees to drive the bar upward from the shoulders while pushing the body underneath. The bar finishes directly overhead with the legs split into a lunge position. The split jerk exercise requires a rapid hip and knee extension to accelerate the bar off the shoulders. The split jerk also involves a forceful hip and knee thrust so that the bar is actually thrown (or *jerked*) upward, and then caught with extended elbows in the overhead position with the legs split into a lunge position.

Starting Position

- Use the power or hang power clean exercise to lift the bar from the floor to the shoulders or remove the bar from a shoulder-height position on a power or squat rack.
- Stand erect with the feet hip-width apart and the toes pointed forward or slightly outward.
- Once the bar is positioned at the front of the shoulders, check to be sure that the grip on the bar is even, pronated, closed, and slightly wider than shoulder-width. The grip should remain relaxed on the bar.
- The elbows should be underneath or slightly ahead of the bar.
- All repetitions begin from this position.

Dip (Active Preparation for the Drive Phase)

- While keeping the torso erect and head in line with the spine, flex the hips and knees at a slow to moderate speed to move the bar in a straight downward path. Do not change the position of the arms.
- The hips should not move backward on the dip. Instead, they should remain directly underneath the shoulders.
- The downward movement is not a full squat, but rather a dip to a depth not to exceed a quarter squat or the catch position of the power clean. Another guideline is a depth that does not exceed 10% of the lifter's body height.

Upward Movement (Drive Phase)

- Immediately upon reaching the lowest position of the dip, reverse the movement by rapidly extending the hips, knees, ankles, and then the elbows to move the bar overhead.
- Initially, the bar needs to be held in place on the shoulders to benefit maximally from the upward momentum produced by the triple extension.
- To reach the split position, rapidly move the feet forward and backward simultaneously, with some separation for balance side to side.
- The neck must slightly hyperextend to allow the bar to pass by the chin (or else the bar will hit the face).

Catch

The drive phase of the split jerk allows the bar to be caught over the head with the elbows fully extended and the legs in the lunge (split) position.

- Catch the bar by rapidly splitting the legs into a lunge position and pushing the body underneath as the bar is still rising from the drive phase.

- The goal is to catch the bar at the same moment the bar reaches maximal height and the feet come back into contact with the floor.

- In comparison to the starting position, the feet move into a slightly wider stance while in the lunge position when coming back into contact with the floor.

- Upon regaining contact with the floor, the front foot is flat and the heel of the back foot is up off the floor.

- The shin of the front leg and the thigh of the back leg should be nearly perpendicular to the floor. The proper length of the split and foot positioning can be determined by these angles.

- The torso should be erect, with the head in line with the spine directly under the bar; the eyes are focused forward.

SPLIT JERK

| Starting position | Dip | Upward movement |

Recovery

▸ After gaining control and balance, stand erect by stepping backward half the distance of the split with the front foot, and then stepping forward half the distance of the split with the back foot. The feet should come parallel to meet in the middle of the distance of the split.

▸ Hold the bar in its final position directly above the head, shoulders, hips, knees, and ankles, all of which are vertically aligned.

Downward Movement

▸ At the completion of the repetition, lower the bar by gradually reducing the muscular tension of the arms to allow a controlled descent of the bar to the shoulders. The hips and knees are simultaneously flexed to cushion the impact of the bar on the shoulders.

▸ If additional repetitions are to be performed, stand fully erect first and then follow the guidelines described for the dip phase. Do not return the bar to the floor between repetitions.

▸ At the completion of the set, first lower the bar from the shoulders to the thighs, then to the floor (similar to the power clean exercise). The bar can also be placed back on the power or squat rack.

TOTAL BODY

| Catch | Recovery—Front foot back | Recovery—Back foot forward |

LOWER BODY

PART II

Hip and Thigh (Multijoint) Exercises

Name	Description of the concentric action	PREDOMINANT MUSCLES INVOLVED	
		Muscle group or body area	Muscles
Front squat	Hip extension	Gluteals	Gluteus maximus
		Hamstrings	Semimembranosus
			Semitendinosus
			Biceps femoris
	Knee extension	Quadriceps	Vastus lateralis
			Vastus intermedius
			Vastus medialis
			Rectus femoris
Back squat	Hip extension	Gluteals	Gluteus maximus
		Hamstrings	Semimembranosus
			Semitendinosus
			Biceps femoris
	Knee extension	Quadriceps	Vastus lateralis
			Vastus intermedius
			Vastus medialis
			Rectus femoris
Romanian deadlift (RDL) (snatch or clean grip)	Hip extension	Gluteals	Gluteus maximus
		Hamstrings	Semimembranosus
			Semitendinosus
			Biceps femoris
Deadlift	Same as the front and back squat		
Hip sled (machine)	Same as the front and back squat		
Seated leg press (machine)	Same as the front and back squat		
Step-up	Same as the front and back squat		
Forward step lunge	Same as the front and back squat, but with these additions:		
	Hip flexion	Hip flexors (of the trailing leg)	Rectus femoris
			Iliopsoas
	Ankle plantar flexion	Calf (of the leading leg)	Soleus
			Gastrocnemius
Glute ham raise	Knee flexion	Hamstrings	Semimembranosus
			Semitendinosus
			Biceps femoris
	Hip extension	Gluteals	Gluteus maximus
	Spinal extension	Spinal erectors*	Erector spinae

The icon denotes an exercise that requires a spotter.

*Many references consider the spinal erectors stabilizers for this exercise.

LOWER BODY

2.1 FRONT SQUAT

Video 2.1

Starting Position: Lifter

▶ With the bar positioned at approximately armpit height on the supporting pins or ledge of a shoulder-high rack stand (or in a power or squat rack), move toward the bar and position the front of the shoulders, hips, and feet directly under the bar.

▶ Grasp the bar using one of the following hand/arm positions:

The most common position is the *clean* or *parallel-arm* position:

- Grasp the bar evenly with a closed and pronated grip, slightly wider than shoulder-width apart.

- Rotate the arms around the bar to place the bar on top of the anterior deltoids and clavicles. The backs of the hands should be either slightly on top of *or* just outside of the shoulders, right next to where the bar rests on the deltoids.

Parallel-arm position

Crossed-arm position

Lowest squat position

Starting positions with parallel-arm position

Downward movement positions

- Raise the elbows to lift the upper arms to parallel with the floor. The wrists should be hyperextended and the elbows fully flexed.

An alternative position is the *crossed-arm* position:

- Flex the elbows and cross the arms in front of the chest.
- Move the body to position the bar evenly on the anterior deltoids without touching it with the hands.
- After the body is in the correct position, place the hands on top of the bar and use pressure from the fingers to keep it in position. Note that this is an open grip; the thumb will not be able to encircle the bar because the shoulders will be in the way.
- Raise the elbows to lift the upper arms to a position parallel to the floor.

- For either hand position, keep the elbows lifted up and forward. This contributes greatly to securing the bar on the shoulders.
- Signal the spotters for assistance, extend the hips and knees to lift the bar off the supporting pins or ledge, and then take a step backward. Be aware of the frame of the rack. If performing the front squat on the inside of a four-pole, boxed type of rack, there may be only about 12 to 18 inches (30 to 46 cm) of space for the backward step. Leave enough room (front to back) so that the bar will not strike the frame during the exercise.

Upward movement positions

Racking the bar

- Position the feet between hip- and shoulder-width apart with the toes pointed slightly outward so the knees track directly over the feet.
- Stand with an erect torso by positioning the shoulders back, tilting the head slightly back, and protruding the chest up and out to create a neutral or slightly arched back.
- All repetitions begin from this position.

Starting Position: Two Spotters

- Stand erect at opposite ends of the bar with the feet shoulder-width apart and the knees slightly flexed.
- Grasp the end of the bar by wrapping the hands around the bar with the thumbs crossed and palms facing the barbell.
- At the lifter's signal, assist with lifting and balancing the bar as it is moved off the supporting pins or ledge.
- Move sideways in unison with the lifter as the lifter steps backward.
- Release the bar smoothly.
- Hold the hands 2 to 3 inches (5 to 8 cm) below the ends of the bar.
- After the lifter is in position, assume a shoulder-width stance with the knees slightly flexed and the torso erect.

Downward Movement: Lifter

- Begin the exercise by flexing the hips and knees slowly and under control.
- Maintain a neutral or slightly arched back and rigid-arm position; do not round the upper back or lean forward as the bar is lowered.
- Focus the eyes ahead and slightly above horizontal, and tilt the head back slightly.
- Keep the body's weight over the middle and heel area of the feet; do not allow the heels to rise off the floor during the descent.
- As the knees flex, keep them aligned over the feet.
- Continue the downward movement until one of these three events occurs (they determine the maximum range of motion, or the lowest squat position):
    1. The thighs are parallel to the floor (if achievable).
    2. The torso begins to round or flex forward.
    3. The heels rise off the floor.
- Actual squat depth is dependent on lower body joint flexibility.
- Keep the body tight and in control; do not bounce, or relax the legs or torso at the bottom of the movement.

Downward Movement: Two Spotters

- Keep the thumbs crossed and hands close to—but not touching—the bar as it descends.
- Slightly flex the knees, hips, and torso, and keep the back neutral when following the path of the bar.

Upward Movement: Lifter

▶ Raise the bar under control by extending the hips and knees.

▶ Maintain a neutral or slightly arched back and rigid-arm position. As the bar is raised, resist the tendency to lean forward by keeping the head tilted slightly back and the chest held up and out.

▶ Move the bar upward by pushing up through the whole foot with the body's weight evenly distributed between the heel and midfoot to keep each foot in contact with the floor and the hips under the bar. Do not allow the body's weight to shift forward onto the balls of the feet.

▶ Keep the knees aligned over the feet; do not allow the knees to shift inward or outward as they extend.

▶ Continue raising the bar at an even rate until the hips and the knees are fully extended to return to the starting position.

▶ At the completion of the set, signal the spotters for assistance to rack the bar, but keep a grip on the bar until both ends are secure and motionless on the supporting pins or ledge.

Upward Movement: Two Spotters

▶ Keep the thumbs crossed and hands close to—but not touching—the bar as it ascends.

▶ Slightly extend the knees, hips, and torso, and keep the back neutral when following the path of the bar.

▶ At the lifter's signal after the set is completed, move sideways in unison with the lifter back to the rack.

▶ Simultaneously grasp the bar and assist with balancing the bar as it is placed back on the supporting pins or ledge.

▶ Release the bar smoothly.

LOWER BODY

2.2   BACK SQUAT

Video 2.2

Starting Position: Lifter

▶ With the bar positioned at approximately armpit height on the supporting pins or ledge of a shoulder-high rack stand (or in a power or squat rack), move toward the bar and position the base of the neck (or upper midback), the hips, and the feet directly under the bar.

▶ Grasp the bar using one of the following bar placement positions:

To perform the back squat with a *low bar* placement, do the following:

- Place the bar evenly *on top of* the posterior deltoids at the middle of the trapezius.
- Grasp the bar evenly with a closed and pronated grip, wider than shoulder-width apart. For most people, the hand placement is wide to compensate for the lower bar position.

High bar position

Low bar position

Lowest squat position

Starting positions with high bar position

Downward movement positions

- An alternative grip is an open grip, which may be more comfortable for the wrists. If an open grip is used, be aware that it does not provide as much control of the bar as a closed grip.

To perform the back squat with a *high bar* placement, do the following:

- Place the bar evenly above the posterior deltoids at the base of the neck.
- Grasp the bar evenly with a closed and pronated grip, slightly wider than shoulder-width apart.

For either bar placement, raise the elbows to create a shelf with the upper back and shoulder muscles for the bar to rest on (a high elbow position also allows the arms to maintain pressure on the bar to prevent it from sliding down the back).

Signal the spotters for assistance, extend the hips and knees to lift the bar off the supporting pins or ledge, and then take a step backward. Be aware of the frame of the rack. If performing the back squat on the inside of a four-pole, boxed type of rack, there may be only about 12 to 18 inches (30 to 46 cm) of space for the backward step. Leave enough room (front to back) so that the bar will not strike the frame during the exercise.

Position the feet between hip- and shoulder-width a[...] pointed slightly outward so the knees track direct[...]

Upward movement positions

Racking the bar

▶ Stand with an erect torso by positioning the shoulders back, tilting the head slightly back, and protruding the chest up and out to create a neutral or slightly arched back.

▶ All repetitions begin from this position.

Starting Position: Two Spotters

▶ Stand erect at opposite ends of the bar with the feet shoulder-width apart and the knees slightly flexed.

▶ Grasp the end of the bar by wrapping the hands around the bar with the thumbs crossed and palms facing the barbell.

▶ At the lifter's signal, assist with lifting and balancing the bar as it is moved off the supporting pins or ledge.

▶ Move sideways in unison with the lifter as the lifter steps backward.

▶ Release the bar smoothly.

▶ Hold the hands 2 to 3 inches (5 to 8 cm) below the ends of the bar.

▶ After the lifter is in position, assume a shoulder-width stance with the knees slightly flexed and the torso erect.

Downward Movement: Lifter

▶ Begin the exercise by flexing the hips and knees slowly and under control.

▶ Maintain a neutral or slightly arched back and high elbow position; do not round the upper back or lean forward as the bar is lowered.

▶ Focus the eyes ahead and slightly above horizontal, and tilt the head back slightly.

▶ Keep the body's weight over the middle and heel area of the feet; do not allow the heels to rise off the floor during the descent.

▶ Keep the knees aligned over the feet as the knees flex.

▶ Continue the downward movement until one of these three events occurs (they determine the maximum range of motion, or the lowest squat position):

  1. The thighs are parallel to the floor (if achievable).
  2. The torso begins to round or flex forward.
  3. The heels rise off the floor.

▶ Actual squat depth is dependent on lower body joint flexibility.

▶ Keep the body tight and in control; do not bounce, or relax the legs or torso at the bottom of the movement.

Downward Movement: Two Spotters

▶ Keep the thumbs crossed and hands close to—but not touching—the bar as it descends.

▶ Slightly flex the knees, hips, and torso, and keep the back neutral when following the path of the bar.

Upward Movement: Lifter

- Raise the bar under control by extending the hips and knees.

- Maintain a neutral or slightly arched back and high elbow position. As the bar is raised, resist the tendency to lean forward by keeping the head tilted slightly back and the chest up and out.

- Move the bar upward by pushing up through the whole foot with the body's weight evenly distributed between the heels and midfoot to keep the feet in contact with the floor and the hips under the bar. Do not allow the body's weight to shift forward onto the balls of the feet.

- Keep the knees aligned over the feet; do not allow the knees to shift inward or outward as they extend.

- Continue raising the bar at an even rate until the hips and knees are fully extended to return to the starting position.

- At the completion of the set, signal the spotters for assistance to rack the bar, but keep a grip on the bar until both ends are secure and motionless on the supporting pins or ledge.

Upward Movement: Two Spotters

- Keep the thumbs crossed and hands close to—but not touching—the bar as it ascends.

- Slightly extend the knees, hips, and torso, and keep the back neutral when following the path of the bar.

- At the lifter's signal after the set is completed, move sideways in unison with the lifter's back to the rack.

- Simultaneously grasp the bar and assist with balancing the bar as it is placed back on the supporting pins or ledge.

- Release the bar smoothly.

2.3 ROMANIAN DEADLIFT (RDL)

Video 2.3

Starting Position

▶ Grasp the bar with a closed, pronated grip. This can be done using the clean grip or the snatch grip.

▶ Follow the starting position and upward movement guidelines of the deadlift exercise (see exercise 2.4) to get in the correct starting position for this exercise, but with one important exception: The knees are slightly flexed and remain in this position throughout the downward and upward movements.

▶ All repetitions begin from this position.

Clean grip   Snatch grip

Starting position

Downward and upward movements

Downward Movement

- Begin the downward movement by lowering the bar slowly, making sure that the bar remains as close as possible to the body.
- As the bar is lowered, the hips flex and move backward.
- Keep the arms straight and relaxed to allow the lower body to handle the load.
- The knees remain slightly flexed as the hips move backward.
- The shoulders move forward as the hips move backward and remain directly over, or in front of, the bar.
- The balance of the foot (center of mass) starts in the midfoot and, as the bar is lowered, begins to move toward the heel.
- Lower the bar just below the knees to the tibial tuberosity, or until a neutral spine cannot be maintained.

Upward Movement

- Once the bar reaches its lowest point, extend the hips to begin the upward movement.
- The bar should remain as close to the body as possible.
- The hips move forward as they extend, while the shoulders move backward as the torso moves toward the vertical position.
- Keep the arms straight and relaxed to allow the lower body to handle the load.
- The balance of the foot (center of mass) starts in the heel, and as the bar is raised, begins to move toward the midfoot.
- Continue the upward movement until the body reaches the starting position.

2.4 DEADLIFT

Video 2.4

Starting Position

The initial position for this exercise is identical to that of the power clean. A common grip variation has one hand that is supinated and the other that is pronated. (Typically, the hand that is pronated is the dominant hand.) This hand position is called an *alternated* grip. This grip is not required to perform the exercise; it simply improves the ability to hold on to the bar with heavier loads. Some people, however, still use a two-hand pronated grip but use wrist straps for an improved grasp on the bar. The photos show a typical pronated grip.

- Squat down with the hips lower than the shoulders (farther than shown in the first photo and video clip) and grasp the bar evenly (more so than shown in the photos and video) with a closed grip shoulder-width (or slightly wider) apart.

- Position the feet between hip- and shoulder-width apart with the toes pointed slightly outward so the knees track directly over the feet.

- Position the arms outside of the knees with the elbows fully extended and pointing out to the sides.

- Position the bar approximately 1 inch (3 cm) in front of the shins and over the balls of the feet.

| Starting position | Middle position | End position |

- Just before liftoff, observe the preparatory body position and lifting guidelines to place the body in the correct position to lift the bar off the floor. Exact positions of the torso, hips, knees, and bar are related to body segment length and lower body joint flexibility.

- All repetitions begin from this position.

Upward Movement

- Begin the exercise by extending the knees and hips slowly and under control. Keep the torso angle constant in relation to the floor; do not let the hips rise before or faster than the shoulders, and keep the back neutral or slightly arched.

- Maintain full elbow extension, with the head neutral in relation to the spine, and the shoulders over or slightly ahead of the bar.

- During the ascent, keep the bar as close to the shins as possible and slightly shift the body's weight back toward the heels.

- As soon as the bar rises to just above the knees, shift the body's weight forward toward the balls of the feet, keeping the heels on the floor.

- Maintain a neutral or slightly arched back, with the elbows fully extended and pointing out to the sides, the shoulders over or slightly ahead of the bar, and the head neutral in relation to the spine.

- Continue to extend the hips and knees until the body reaches a fully erect torso position.

Downward Movement

- Slowly flex the hips and knees at the same rate to return the bar to the floor in a controlled manner.

- During the descent, keep the bar as close to the thighs and shins as possible.

- Maintain a neutral or slightly arched back, with the elbows fully extended and pointing out to the sides, the shoulders over or slightly ahead of the bar, and the head neutral in relation to the spine.

- Touch the plates to the floor, and then immediately (without a pause) lift the bar back up for the next repetition.

LOWER BODY

2.5   HIP SLED (MACHINE)

Video 2.5

Starting Position

- Sit inside the machine with the head, back, hips, and buttocks pressed evenly against their respective pads (i.e., in the center of the pads, not to the left or right side). Some machines have shoulder pads that allow the lifter to wedge the shoulders underneath the pads.

- All body segments other than the legs must be firmly positioned against their pads to provide maximal support to the spine and low back. If the angle of the back pad is adjustable, move it up or down to allow the torso and legs to form approximately a 90-degree angle (at the hips) when the feet are properly positioned on the foot platform and the knees are fully extended.

- Place the feet between hip- and shoulder-width apart and flat on the foot platform with the toes pointed slightly outward. Both feet must be positioned in the same manner—the same space should be seen between the left foot and the left side of the foot platform as there is between the right foot and the right side of the foot platform. Also, both feet should have an identical toed-out angle.

- Position the thighs and lower legs parallel to each other.

Foot position

Starting position

Downward and upward movements

- Grasp the handles or the machine frame and simultaneously extend the hips and knees to raise the foot platform 1 to 2 inches (3 to 5 cm).
- Keep the hips and buttocks on the seat and the back pressed firmly and evenly against the back pad as the foot platform rises.
- Remove the support mechanism from the foot platform. Many varieties of mechanisms exist, but most require one or two handles near the body to be turned outward or moved.
- Grasp the handles or the machine frame again after removing the support mechanism to help keep the body firmly in place.
- Extend the hips and knees—but do not lock out the knees—to raise the foot platform to the starting position.
- Maintain a stationary lower body as it braces the foot platform.
- All repetitions begin from this position.

Downward Movement

- Begin the exercise by flexing the hips and knees slowly and under control.
- Keep the hips and buttocks on the seat and the back pressed firmly and evenly against the back pad.
- Keep the thighs and lower legs parallel to each other; any deviations will place undue stress on the low back and knees. Keep the knees aligned over the feet as they flex.
- Continue the downward movement until one of these four events occurs (they determine the maximum range of motion, or the bottom position):
    1. The thighs are parallel to the foot platform (if achievable).
    2. The buttocks lose contact with the seat.
    3. The hips roll off the back pad.
    4. The heels rise off the foot platform.
- The extent of the range of motion depends on the degree of spinal, hip, knee, and ankle flexibility as well as the machine's design features and adjustment capabilities.
- At the bottom of the movement, do not relax the legs or torso, and do not bounce the foot platform to spring it back up for the next repetition.

Upward Movement

- Push the foot platform up and under control by extending the hips and knees. The feet should remain flat on the foot platform.
- Keep the hips and buttocks on the seat and the back pressed firmly and evenly against the back pad. Do not shift the hips or allow the buttocks to lose contact with the seat.
- Keep the thighs and lower legs parallel to each other; do not allow the knees to shift inward or outward as they extend.
- Continue pushing the foot platform up until the knees are fully extended but not forcefully locked.
- At the completion of the set, slightly flex the hips and knees, return the support mechanism back into place, lower the foot platform until it is resting on the supports, and then stand up and step out of the machine.

LOWER BODY

2.6   SEATED LEG PRESS (MACHINE)

Video 2.6

Starting Position

▶ Sit in the machine with the head, back, hips, and buttocks pressed evenly against their respective pads (i.e., in the center of the pads, not to the left or right side).

▶ All body segments other than the legs must be firmly positioned against their pads to provide maximal support to the spine and low back. If the horizontal position of the foot platform or the seat is adjustable, move it forward or backward to allow the thighs to be parallel to the foot platform when sitting in the starting position.

▶ Place the feet between hip- and shoulder-width apart and flat on the foot platform with the toes pointed slightly outward. Both feet must be positioned in the same manner—the same space should be seen between the left foot and the left side of the foot platform as there is between the right foot and the right side of the foot platform. Also, both feet should have an identical toed-out angle.

▶ Position the legs parallel to each other.

▶ Grasp the handles or the sides of the seat.

▶ All repetitions begin from this position.

Starting position   Forward and backward movements

Forward Movement

- Begin the exercise by extending the hips and knees slowly and under control to push the platform forward. (Note that in some machines, the platform is fixed and the seat will move backward during this phase.) The feet should remain flat on the foot platform.

- Keep the head, shoulders, back, hips, and buttocks pressed evenly against their respective pads; do not shift the hips or allow the buttocks to lose contact with the seat.

- Keep the legs parallel to each other; do not allow the knees to shift inward or outward as they extend.

- Continue the forward movement until the knees are fully extended but not forcefully locked.

Backward Movement

- Allow the hips and knees to flex slowly to bring the platform back to the starting position.

- Keep the head, shoulders, back, hips, and buttocks pressed evenly against their respective pads.

- Keep the legs parallel to each other; any deviations will place undue stress on the low back and knees. As the knees flex, keep them aligned over the feet.

- Continue flexing the hips and knees until the thighs are parallel to the foot platform.

- At the completion of the set, release the handles or the sides of the seat and step out of the machine.

2.7   STEP-UP

Video 2.7

The box used for this exercise should have a top surface area that allows the lifter's whole foot (shoe) to fit with extra space behind the heel and ahead of the toe. The box should be 12 to 18 inches (30 to 46 cm) high, or high enough to create a 90-degree angle at the knee and hip joints when the lead foot is on the box. Also, the box should be placed on a non-slip floor and have a nonslip top surface. *Note:* To allow an optimal view of the exercise technique, a power or squat rack is not shown.

Starting Position: Lifter

▸ With the bar positioned at approximately armpit height on the out-side of a power or squat rack, move toward the bar and position the base of the neck (or upper midback) and the hips and feet directly under the bar.

▸ Place the bar evenly above the posterior deltoids at the base of the neck (as seen in the high bar position in the back squat exercise).

▸ Grasp the bar evenly with a closed and pronated grip, slightly wider than shoulder-width apart.

Starting positions   Initial contact of lead foot with top of box

▶ Raise the elbows to create a shelf with the upper back and shoulder muscles for the bar to rest on (a high elbow position also allows the arms to maintain pressure on the bar to prevent it from sliding down the back).

▶ Signal the spotter for assistance and then extend the hips and knees to lift the bar off the supporting pins or ledge. Move to a spot near the front of the box.

▶ Place the feet hip-width apart with the toes pointed ahead.

▶ All repetitions begin from this position.

Starting Position: Spotter

▶ Stand erect and close behind the lifter (but not so close as to be a distraction).

▶ Place the feet shoulder-width apart with the knees slightly flexed.

▶ At the lifter's signal, assist with lifting and balancing the bar as it is moved out of the rack.

▶ Move in unison with the lifter as the lifter moves to the starting position.

Middle of upward movement positions

Completion of upward movement positions

▶ After the lifter is in position, assume a hip-width stance with the knees slightly flexed and the torso erect.

▶ Position the hands near the lifter's hips, waist, or torso.

Upward Movement: Lifter

▶ Begin the exercise by stepping up with one leg (the lead leg). The initial contact of the lead foot with the top of the box must be made by the entire foot; do not allow the heel to hang off the edge of the box.

▶ Keep the torso erect; do not lean forward.

▶ Keep the trailing foot in the starting position, but shift the body's weight to the lead leg.

▶ Forcefully extend the lead hip and knee to move the body up and on top of the box; do not push off or hop up with the trailing leg or foot.

▶ As the hip and knee of the lead leg fully extend to a standing position on top of the box, bring the trailing foot up and place it next to the lead foot.

▶ At the highest position, stand erect and pause before beginning the downward movement.

Upward Movement: Spotter

▶ Take a small step forward with the lead leg as the lifter steps up on the box.

▶ As the lifter reaches the highest position, bring the trailing leg forward to be next to the lead leg.

▶ Keep the hands as near as possible to the lifter's hips, waist, or torso.

▶ Assist only when necessary to keep the lifter balanced.

Downward Movement: Lifter

▶ Shift the body's weight to the same lead leg.

▶ Step off the box with the same trailing leg.

▶ Maintain an erect torso position.

▶ Place the trailing foot on the floor the same distance from the box as the starting position.

▶ When the trailing foot is in full contact with the floor, shift the body's weight to the trailing leg.

▶ Step off the box with the lead leg.

▶ Bring the lead foot back to a position next to the trailing foot.

▶ Stand erect in the starting position, pause to gain full balance, and then alternate lead legs and repeat the movement with the new lead leg (some lifters may benefit from repeating the action words "up-up-down-down" during the set to help perform the exercise correctly).

▶ At the completion of the set, signal the spotter for assistance to rack the bar, but keep a grip on the bar until both ends are secure and motionless on the supporting pins or ledge.

Downward Movement: Spotter

- Take a small step backward with the same trailing leg as the lifter steps back down to the floor.
- As the lifter steps off the box with the lead leg, take a step backward with the same lead leg.
- Keep the hands near the lifter's hips, waist, or torso.
- Stand erect in the starting position, pause to wait for the lifter, and alternate lead legs.
- Assist only when necessary to keep the lifter balanced.
- At the lifter's signal after the set is completed, help the lifter rack the bar.

2.8 FORWARD STEP LUNGE

Video 2.8

This exercise can be performed in a variety of ways in many directions. For many people, performing this exercise with only the body as the weight is enough. Well-trained lifters can use a bar (as explained in the following section) for additional resistance. An alternative is to hold a pair of dumbbells at the sides; this is especially helpful if balancing a bar across the shoulders is too difficult or if an experienced spotter is not available. In any situation, a large (or at least long) floor space is required for this exercise. *Note:* To allow an optimal view of the exercise technique, a power or squat rack is not shown.

Starting Position: Lifter

▶ With the bar positioned at approximately armpit height on the outside of a power or squat rack, move toward the bar and position the base of the neck (or upper midback) and the hips and feet directly under the bar.

▶ Place the bar evenly above the posterior deltoids at the base of the neck (as seen in the high bar position in the back squat exercise).

Starting positions   Beginning of forward movement positions

- Grasp the bar evenly with a closed and pronated grip, slightly wider than shoulder-width apart.

- Raise the elbows to create a shelf with the upper back and shoulder muscles for the bar to rest on (a high elbow position also allows the arms to maintain pressure on the bar to prevent it from sliding down the back).

- Signal the spotter for assistance, and then extend the hips and knees to lift the bar off the supporting pins or ledge. Take two or three steps backward.

- Place the feet hip-width apart with the toes pointed ahead.

- All repetitions begin from this position.

Starting Position: Spotter

- Stand erect and close behind the lifter (but not close enough to be a distraction).

- Place the feet shoulder-width apart with the knees slightly flexed.

- At the lifter's signal, assist with lifting and balancing the bar as it is moved out of the rack.

Completion of forward movement positions

Middle of backward movement positions

▶ Move in unison with the lifter as the lifter moves backward to the starting position.

▶ After the lifter is in position, assume a hip-width stance with the knees slightly flexed and the torso erect.

▶ Position the hands near the lifter's hips, waist, or torso.

Forward Movement: Lifter

▶ Begin the exercise by taking one exaggerated step directly forward with one leg; this leg is called the lead leg.

▶ Keep the torso erect and arms tight as the lead foot moves forward and contacts the floor. The trailing foot remains in its starting position, but as the lead leg steps forward, balance shifts to the ball of the trailing foot and the trailing knee flexes slightly.

▶ Plant the lead foot flat on the floor with the toes pointing ahead or slightly inward. To help maintain balance, this foot needs to be placed directly ahead from its initial position, and the lead ankle, knee, and hip must be in one vertical plane. Do not step slightly to the right or left, or allow the knee to shift in or out.

▶ After balance has shifted to both feet and stability is achieved, flex the lead knee to lower the trailing knee toward the floor.

▶ The torso must stay erect, with the shoulders held back and the head facing forward. Sit back on the trailing leg; do not lean forward or look down.

▶ The lowest ideal body position is with the trailing knee 1 to 2 inches (3 to 5 cm) away from the floor, the lead knee flexed to about 90 degrees, the lead lower leg perpendicular to the floor, and the lead foot flat on the floor. The lead knee must not extend past the toes of the lead foot. Actual lunge depth depends primarily on hip joint flexibility, especially in the iliopsoas muscles.

▶ Allow the ankle of the trailing foot to fully dorsiflex with the toes fully extended.

Forward Movement: Spotter

▶ Step forward with the same lead leg as the lifter.

▶ Keep the lead knee and foot aligned with the lifter's lead knee and foot.

▶ Plant the lead foot 12 to 18 inches (30 to 46 cm) behind the lifter's lead foot.

▶ Flex the lead knee as the lifter's lead knee flexes.

▶ Keep the torso erect.

▶ Keep the hands near the lifter's hips, waist, or torso.

▶ Assist only when necessary to keep the lifter balanced.

Backward Movement: Lifter

- Shift the balance forward to the lead foot and forcefully push off the floor with the lead foot by plantar flexing the ankle of the lead foot and by extending the lead knee and hip joints. Do not jerk the upper body back; maintain its vertical position.

- As the lead foot moves back toward the trailing foot, balance will shift back to the trailing foot. This will cause the heel of the trailing foot to regain contact with the floor.

- Move the lead foot back to place it next to the trailing foot. Do not stutter-step backward.

- As the lead foot is placed flat on the floor in its starting position, evenly divide the body's weight over both feet. The torso should be erect, similar to the starting position.

- Stand erect in the starting position, pause to gain full balance, and then alternate lead legs and repeat the movement with the new lead leg.

- Some lifters may benefit from dividing the movement into smaller portions during the repetition to help perform the exercise correctly:

  1. Step forward.
  2. Plant the lead foot.
  3. Lunge down and back.
  4. Stand up.
  5. Push off.

- At the completion of the set, signal the spotter for assistance to rack the bar, but keep a grip on the bar until both ends are secure and motionless on the supporting pins or ledge.

Backward Movement: Spotter

- Push backward with the lead leg in unison with the lifter.

- Bring the lead foot back to a position next to the trailing foot; do not stutter-step backward.

- Keep the hands near the lifter's hips, waist, or torso.

- Stand erect in the starting position, pause to wait for the lifter, and alternate lead legs for the next repetition.

- Assist only when necessary to keep the lifter balanced.

- At the lifter's signal after the set is completed, help the lifter rack the bar.

2.9   GLUTE HAM RAISE

Starting Position

▸ To begin, position the body on the glute ham bench with the ankles between the ankle roller pads, the feet flat against the foot platform, and the thighs (just above the knees) pressed against the pad.

▸ Flex the knees to approximately 90 degrees to position the upper body perpendicular to the floor.

▸ The shoulders, hips, and knees should be vertically aligned with the head in a neutral position.

▸ Cross the arms in front of the chest.

Downward Movement

▸ Begin the downward movement by slowly allowing the knees to extend.

▸ The shoulders, hips, and knees remain aligned, with the arms still crossed in front of the chest.

Starting position   Parallel position

- As the aligned torso and thighs approach parallel to the floor, allow the hips to flex and the knees to fully extend. Doing so will allow the thighs to move up on the thigh pad so the hips can flex over the top of the pad. When this occurs, the upper body can continue moving down until it is nearly perpendicular to the floor.

- At the lowest point, the shoulders and hips are still aligned with the head in a neutral position.

Upward Movement

- Begin the upward movement by extending the hips.

- Maintain alignment of the hips and shoulders.

- When the torso and thighs are parallel to the floor, flex the knees to allow the thighs to move down on the thigh pad so the hips can extend over the top of the pad.

- Continue extending the hips and flexing the knees to approximately a 90-degree angle to move the upper body back to the starting position.

Lowest position

Hip and Thigh (Single-Joint) Exercises

Name	Description of the concentric action	PREDOMINANT MUSCLES INVOLVED	
		Muscle group or body area	Muscles
Stiff-leg deadlift	Hip extension	Gluteals	Gluteus maximus
		Hamstrings	Semimembranosus
			Semitendinosus
			Biceps femoris
	Spinal extension	Spinal erectors*	Erector spinae
Good morning	Hip extension	Hamstrings	Semimembranosus
			Semitendinosus
			Biceps femoris
		Gluteals	Gluteus maximus
	Spinal extension	Spinal erectors*	Erector spinae
Leg (knee) extension (machine)	Knee extension	Quadriceps	Vastus lateralis
			Vastus intermedius
			Vastus medialis
			Rectus femoris
Seated leg (knee) curl (machine)	Knee flexion	Hamstrings	Semimembranosus
			Semitendinosus
			Biceps femoris

*Many references consider the spinal erectors stabilizers for these two exercises.

2.10   STIFF-LEG DEADLIFT

Well-trained lifters may stand on a raised platform to perform this exercise through a greater range of motion. Instead of touching the plates to the floor, the lifter can lower the bar to touch the feet. Note that doing so requires an extremely large degree of flexibility in the hamstrings, gluteals, and low back; therefore, most people should not use a raised platform. Nearly all lifters should stand on the floor and safely lower the bar only to knee or midshin level.

Starting Position

- Observe the preparatory body position and lifting guidelines to place the body in the correct position to lift the bar off the floor.

- Follow the starting position and upward movement guidelines of the deadlift exercise to get in the correct starting position of this exercise, but with one important exception: The knees are slightly flexed and remain in this position throughout the downward and upward movements.

- All repetitions begin from this position.

Starting position

Downward and upward movements

Downward Movement

- Begin the exercise by forming a neutral or slightly arched back, and then flex forward at the hips slowly and under control.

- During the descent, keep the knees in the same slightly flexed position, with the back neutral or slightly arched and the elbows fully extended.

- Continue the downward movement until one of these four events occurs (they determine the maximum range of motion, or the bottom position):

  1. The plates touch the floor (or the bar touches the feet of well-trained lifters standing on a raised platform).
  2. The back cannot be held in the neutral or slightly arched position.
  3. The knees fully extend.
  4. The heels rise off the floor.

- Keep the body tight and in control; do not bounce or relax the torso at the bottom of the movement.

Upward Movement

- Raise the bar by extending the hips.

- During the ascent, keep the knees in the same slightly flexed position with the back neutral or slightly arched and the elbows fully extended.

- Continue the upward movement to return to the starting position.

- At the completion of the set, slowly flex the hips and knees at the same rate (to keep an erect torso position) to squat down and return the bar to the floor in a controlled manner.

2.11   GOOD MORNING

Video 2.11

Starting Position

Note: To allow an optimal view of the exercise technique, a power or squat rack is not shown.

- With the bar positioned at approximately armpit height on the outside of a power or squat rack, move toward the bar and position the base of the neck (or upper midback) and the hips and feet directly under the bar.

- Place the bar evenly above the posterior deltoids at the base of the neck (as seen in the high bar position in the back squat exercise).

- Grasp the bar evenly with a closed and pronated grip, slightly wider than shoulder-width apart.

- Raise the elbows to create a shelf with the upper back and shoulder muscles for the bar to rest on (a high elbow position also allows the arms to maintain pressure on the bar to prevent it from sliding down the back).

Starting position   Downward and upward movements

- To remove the bar from the rack, extend the hips and knees to lift the bar off the supporting pins or ledge and take a few steps backward. (Be aware of any space limitations around the power or squat rack.)

- Position the body with the

  - feet between hip- and shoulder-width apart;
  - knees slightly flexed;
  - toes angled slightly outward (about 10 degrees);
  - torso erect with shoulders back, head tilted slightly back, chest up and out to create a neutral or slightly arched back; and
  - elbows held up to keep the bar in position.

- All repetitions begin from this position.

Downward Movement

- Begin the exercise by flexing the hips slowly and under control. The buttocks should move straight back during the descent and the knees should remain slightly flexed.

- Maintain a neutral or slightly arched back and high elbow position. Focus the eyes ahead and slightly above horizontal, and tilt the head back slightly.

- Do not allow the heels to rise off the floor.

- Continue the downward movement until the torso is parallel to the floor. If unable to achieve the parallel position, continue the exercise only as far as proper technique is maintained.

- Keep the body tight and in control; do not bounce or relax the torso at the bottom of the movement.

Upward Movement

- Raise the bar by extending the hips slowly and under control; keep the knees slightly flexed.

- Maintain a neutral or slightly arched back and high elbow position with the head tilted back.

- Continue the upward movement to return to the starting position.

- At the completion of the set, slowly walk forward and return the bar to the supporting pins or ledge.

2.12   LEG (KNEE) EXTENSION (MACHINE)

Starting Position

▸ Sit erect on the seat with the back and hips pressed evenly against their respective pads (i.e., in the center of the pads, not to the left or right side).

▸ Hook the feet under the roller pad. If it is adjustable, position the pad to be in contact with the insteps of the feet (while in the seated position). Doing so might require someone else to reposition the roller pad, or it might require a trial-and-error approach of sitting in the machine, checking the roller pad, getting out and making adjustments, sitting back down, and rechecking it.

▸ The position in the machine must allow the knees to be in line with the axis of rotation of the machine. If the back pad is adjustable, move it forward or backward to create this alignment.

▸ Position the thighs, lower legs, and feet hip-width apart and parallel to each other.

▸ Grasp the side handles or seat pad.

▸ All repetitions begin from this position.

Starting position

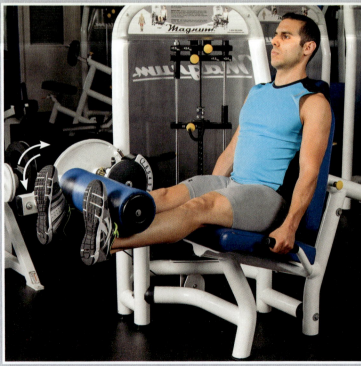

Upward and downward movements

Upward Movement

- Begin the exercise by extending the knees slowly and under control.
- Keep the thighs, lower legs, and feet parallel to each other; do not allow the thighs to shift inward or outward (i.e., internally or externally rotate at the hip) as the knees extend.
- Keep a tight grasp on the handles or seat pad during the ascent to minimize upper body and thigh movement.
- Do not swing the legs or jerk the torso backward to help raise the weight.
- Continue the upward movement until the knees are fully extended but not forcefully locked.

Downward Movement

- Allow the knees to flex to lower the roller pad slowly and under control back to the starting position.
- Do not lower the weight stack uncontrollably.
- Keep the thighs, lower legs, and feet parallel to each other.
- The back and hips should remain in contact with their respective pads.
- At the completion of the set, unhook the feet from under the roller pad and step out of the machine.

Video 2.13

2.13 SEATED LEG (KNEE) CURL (MACHINE)

Starting Position

- Raise the thigh pad to its highest position.

- Sit erect on the seat with the back and hips pressed evenly against their respective pads (i.e., in the center of the pads, not to the left or right side).

- Extend the knees and place the ankles on top of the roller pad. If it is adjustable, position the pad to be in contact with the back of the heels or lower calves, just above the tops of the shoes (when seated). Doing so might require someone else to reposition the roller pad, or it might require a trial-and-error approach of sitting in the machine, checking the roller pad, getting out and making adjustments, sitting back down, and rechecking it.

- The position in the machine must allow the knees to be in line with the axis of rotation of the machine. If the back pad is adjustable, move it forward or backward to create this alignment.

- Position the thighs, lower legs, and feet hip-width apart and parallel to each other.

- Lower the thigh pad so it firmly presses against the thighs.

Starting position

Downward and upward movements

LOWER BODY

- Grasp the side handles or seat pad.
- All repetitions begin from this position.

Downward Movement

- Begin the exercise by flexing the knees slowly and under control.
- Keep the thighs, lower legs, and feet parallel to each other; do not allow the thighs to shift inward or outward (i.e., internally or externally rotate at the hip) as the knees flex.
- Keep a tight grasp on the handles or seat pad to minimize upper body and thigh movement.
- Do not move the upper body or kick back with the legs to help raise the weight.
- Continue the downward movement until the knees are flexed at least 90 degrees. Actual range of motion will depend on the length of the limbs, the flexibility of the quadriceps, and the design of the machine.

Upward Movement

- Allow the knees to extend to raise the roller pad slowly and under control back to the starting position.
- Do not lower the weight stack uncontrollably.
- Keep the thighs, lower legs, and feet parallel to each other.
- The back, hips, and thighs should remain in contact with their respective pads.
- At the completion of the set, raise the thigh pad to the highest position, move the heels off the roller pad, and step out of the machine.

Calf (Single-Joint) Exercises

Name	Description of the concentric action	PREDOMINANT MUSCLES INVOLVED	
		Muscle group or body area	Muscles
Seated calf (heel) raise (machine)	Ankle plantar flexion	Calf	Soleus
			Gastrocnemius
Standing calf (heel) raise (machine)	Same as the seated calf (heel) raise (machine)		Soleus
			Gastrocnemius

LOWER BODY

2.14 SEATED CALF (HEEL) RAISE (MACHINE)

Video 2.14

Starting Position

- Raise the thigh (knee) pad to its highest position.

- Sit erect on the seat and place the balls of the feet (metatarsals) on the nearest edge of the step with the legs and feet hip-width apart and parallel to each other.

- If the seat height is adjustable, position it to place the thighs parallel to the floor (when the feet are in position).

- Lower the thigh (knee) pad so it firmly presses against the front of the lower thigh area (actual contact of the pad depends on the length of the thighs, seat height, and design of the machine).

- Grasp the handles.

- Plantar flex the ankles to raise the thigh (knee) pad 1 to 2 inches (3 to 5 cm).

- Remove the support mechanism. Many varieties exist, but most require a handle near the hands or body to be turned outward or moved.

Starting position

Upward and downward movements

- Slowly allow the heels to lower fully under control to a comfortable, stretched position.
- All repetitions begin from this position.

Upward Movement

- Begin the exercise by plantar flexing the ankles slowly and under control.
- Keep the torso erect and the legs and feet parallel to each other.
- Apply even pressure on all of the metatarsals; do not slightly invert or evert the feet to rise up only on the big or little toes.
- Do not use the arms to pull on the handles or thigh (knee) pad to help raise the weight.
- Continue the upward movement until the calf muscles are fully contracted (i.e., the ankles are fully plantar flexed).

Downward Movement

- Allow the heels to lower slowly and under control back to the starting position.
- At the bottom of the movement, do not bounce the weight to spring it back up for the next repetition.
- At the completion of the set, slightly plantar flex the ankles, return the support back into place, and then stand up and step out of the machine.

LOWER BODY

2.15 STANDING CALF (HEEL) RAISE (MACHINE)

Starting Position

▸ Position the body evenly under the shoulder pads and stand erect. The hips should be under the shoulders with the knees fully extended but not forcefully locked.

▸ Grasp the handles.

▸ Place the balls of the feet (metatarsals) on the nearest edge of the step with the legs and feet hip-width apart and parallel to each other. Reposition the body so the hips are under the shoulders and the knees are fully extended but not forcefully locked.

▸ Slowly allow the heels to lower fully under control to a comfortable, stretched position. (The weight to be lifted should be above its resting position when the heels are in their lowest stretched position. If not, lower the height of the shoulder pads 2 to 3 inches [5 to 8 cm].)

▸ All repetitions begin from this position.

Starting position

Upward and downward movements

Upward Movement

▶ Begin the exercise by plantar flexing the ankles slowly and under control.

▶ Keep the torso erect and the legs and feet parallel to each other.

▶ Apply even pressure on all of the metatarsals; do not slightly invert or evert the feet to rise up only on the big or little toes.

▶ Do not push or swing the hips forward to help raise the weight.

▶ Continue the upward movement until the calf muscles are fully contracted (i.e., the ankles are fully plantar flexed).

Downward Movement

▶ Allow the heels to lower slowly and under control back to the starting position.

▶ At the bottom of the movement, do not bounce the weight to spring it back up for the next repetition.

▶ At the completion of the set, slowly flex the hips and knees to lower the weight to its resting position and then step out of the machine.

UPPER BODY

PART III

Chest (Multijoint) Exercises

Name	Description of the concentric action	PREDOMINANT MUSCLES INVOLVED	
		Muscle group or body area	Muscles
Flat barbell bench press	Shoulder transverse (horizontal) adduction	Chest	Pectoralis major
		Shoulders	Anterior deltoid
	Scapular protraction (abduction)	Scapulae	Serratus anterior
		Chest	Pectoralis minor
	Elbow extension	Upper arm (posterior)	Triceps brachii
Incline barbell bench press	Same as the flat barbell bench press		
Flat dumbbell bench press	Same as the flat barbell bench press		
Incline dumbbell bench press	Same as the flat barbell bench press		
Vertical chest press (machine)	Same as the flat barbell bench press		

The icon denotes an exercise that requires a spotter.

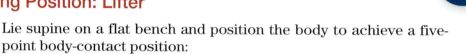

UPPER BODY

3.1   FLAT BARBELL BENCH PRESS

Video 3.1

Starting Position: Lifter

▸ Lie supine on a flat bench and position the body to achieve a five-point body-contact position:

1. The head is placed firmly on the bench.
2. The shoulders and upper back are placed firmly and evenly on the bench.
3. The buttocks are placed evenly on the bench.
4. The right foot is flat on the floor.
5. The left foot is flat on the floor.

▸ Adjust the body on the bench to position the eyes directly below the racked bar.

▸ Grasp the bar evenly with a closed and pronated grip, slightly wider than shoulder-width apart.

▸ Signal the spotter for assistance in moving the bar off the rack to a position over the chest with the elbows fully extended. This is the liftoff. All repetitions begin from this position.

Starting Position: Spotter

▸ Stand erect behind the head of the bench.
▸ Place the feet shoulder-width apart with the knees slightly flexed.

Liftoff

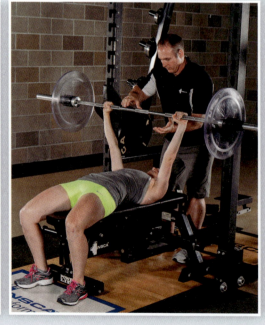

Starting positions

Downward movements

- Grasp the bar with a closed, alternated grip inside the lifter's hands.
- At the lifter's signal, assist with moving the bar off the rack.
- Guide the bar to a position over the lifter's chest.
- Release the bar smoothly.

Downward Movement: Lifter

- Begin the exercise by lowering the bar slowly and under control toward the chest.
- Move the elbows down past the torso and slightly away from the body.
- Keep the wrists stiff and the forearms perpendicular to the floor and parallel to each other. The width of the grip will determine how parallel the forearms are to each other.
- Lower the bar to lightly touch the chest at approximately nipple level; do not bounce the bar on the chest or arch the low back to raise the chest to meet the bar.
- Keep the head, torso, hips, and feet in a five-point body-contact position.

Downward Movement: Spotter

- Keep the hands in the alternated grip position close to—but not touching—the bar as it descends.
- Slightly flex the knees, hips, and torso, and keep the back neutral when following the path of the bar.

Upward movements   Racking the bar

Upward Movement: Lifter

- Press the bar up and slightly backward.
- Maintain the same stationary five-point body-contact position; do not lift the head or arch the low back, and do not lift the buttocks or feet.
- Keep the wrists stiff and the forearms perpendicular to the floor and parallel to each other.
- Continue pressing the bar up until the elbows are fully extended but not forcefully locked.
- At the completion of the set, signal the spotter for assistance to rack the bar, but keep a grip on the bar until both ends are secure and motionless on the supporting pins or ledge.

Upward Movement: Spotter

- Keep the hands in the alternated grip position close to—but not touching—the bar as it ascends.
- Slightly extend the knees, hips, and torso, and keep the back neutral when following the path of the bar.
- At the lifter's signal after the set is completed, grasp the bar with an alternated grip inside the lifter's hands.
- Guide the bar back onto the rack.
- Keep a grip on the bar until it is secure and motionless on the supporting pins or ledge.

3.2 INCLINE BARBELL BENCH PRESS

Video 3.2

Starting Position: Lifter

- Before performing this exercise, check the height of the seat and adjust it to allow for the following conditions:
  - The thighs are approximately parallel to the floor (with the feet flat).
  - The head is lower than the racked bar and resting at the top of the bench.
  - The bar can be lifted off and returned to the supporting pins or ledge without hitting the top of the head (the seat is too high) or requiring the use of the legs to help reach the rack (the seat is too low).

- Sit on the seat of an incline bench and then lean back to place the body in a five-point body-contact position:
  1. The head is placed firmly against the bench.
  2. The shoulders and upper back are placed firmly and evenly against the bench.
  3. The buttocks are placed evenly on the seat.
  4. The right foot is flat on the floor.
  5. The left foot is flat on the floor.

- Grasp the bar evenly with a closed and pronated grip, slightly wider than shoulder-width apart.

- Signal the spotter for assistance in moving the bar off the rack to a position over the neck and face with the elbows fully extended. This is the liftoff. All repetitions begin from this position.

Starting Position: Spotter

- Stand erect behind the head of the bench.
- Place the feet shoulder-width apart with the knees slightly flexed.
- Grasp the bar with a closed, alternated grip inside the lifter's hands.
- At the lifter's signal, assist with moving the bar off the rack.
- Guide the bar to a position over the lifter's neck and face.
- Release the bar smoothly.

Downward Movement: Lifter

- Begin the exercise by lowering the bar slowly and under control. It will have a tendency to move away from the body, depending on the angle of the bench, but guide it toward the upper chest area.
- Move the elbows down past the torso and slightly away from the body.

▸ Keep the wrists stiff and the forearms perpendicular to the floor and parallel to each other. The width of the grip will determine how parallel the forearms are to each other.

▸ Lower the bar to lightly touch the chest at approximately the upper one-third of the chest, between the clavicles and the nipples; do not bounce the bar on the chest or arch the low back to raise the chest to meet the bar.

▸ Keep the head, torso, hips, and feet in a five-point body-contact position.

Downward Movement: Spotter

▸ Keep the hands in the alternated grip position close to—but not touching—the bar as it descends.

▸ Slightly flex the knees, hips, and torso, and keep the back neutral when following the path of the bar.

Upward Movement: Lifter

▸ Press the bar upward and slightly backward. To keep it from falling forward (because of the angled torso position), press the bar up so it passes close by the face as opposed to out away from the chest.

INCLINE BARBELL BENCH PRESS

Starting positions

Downward and upward movements

- Do not arch the low back, raise the hips, or push up with the legs (by trying to stand up); the body and feet should not move from their initial positions.

- Keep the wrists stiff and the forearms perpendicular to the floor and parallel to each other.

- Continue pressing the bar up until the elbows are fully extended but not forcefully locked.

- At the completion of the set, signal the spotter for assistance to rack the bar, but keep a grip on the bar until both ends are secure and motionless on the supporting pins or ledge.

Upward Movement: Spotter

- Keep the hands in the alternated grip position close to—but not touching—the bar as it ascends.

- Slightly extend the knees, hips, and torso, and keep the back neutral when following the path of the bar.

- At the lifter's signal after the set is completed, grasp the bar with an alternated grip inside the lifter's hands.

- Guide the bar back onto the rack.

- Keep a grip on the bar until it is secure and motionless on the supporting pins or ledge.

3.3   FLAT DUMBBELL BENCH PRESS

Video 3.3

Starting Position: Lifter

▸ Grasp two dumbbells of equal weight with a closed grip. Position the outside surface of the bottom half of the dumbbells against the front of the thighs (the dumbbell handles will be parallel to each other).

▸ Sit on one end of a flat bench with the dumbbells resting on the thighs.

▸ Lie back so the head rests on the other end of the bench. Once the supine position is achieved, first move the dumbbells to the chest (armpit) area and then signal the spotter for assistance in moving them to a position above the chest with the elbows extended and the forearms parallel to each other.

▸ Reposition the head, shoulders, buttocks, and feet to achieve a five-point body-contact position:

1. The head is placed firmly on the bench.
2. The shoulders and upper back are placed firmly and evenly on the bench.
3. The buttocks are placed evenly on the bench.
4. The right foot is flat on the floor.
5. The left foot is flat on the floor.

Starting positions

Downward and upward movements

- The most common dumbbell position is with the dumbbell handles in line with each other with the palms facing toward the feet. Another option is to hold the dumbbells in a neutral position (i.e., parallel to each other with the palms facing each other).

- All repetitions begin from this extended-elbow position with the dumbbells supported over the chest.

Starting Position: Spotter

- Get into a low (but still erect) body position close to the head of the bench.

- To create a stable spotting position, get into a fully lunged position with one knee on the floor and the foot of the other leg ahead of the rear knee and flat on the floor.

- Grasp the lifter's forearms near the wrists.

- At the lifter's signal, assist with moving the dumbbells to a position over the lifter's chest.

- Release the lifter's forearms smoothly.

Downward Movement: Lifter

- Begin the exercise by lowering the dumbbells slowly and under control toward the chest. To maintain a stable body position on the bench, lower the dumbbells at the same rate.

- Keep the wrists stiff, the forearms perpendicular to the floor, and the dumbbell handles in line with each other (unless using a neutral grip). Minimize all forward-to-backward and side-to-side movement.

- Guide the dumbbells down and slightly out to the lateral side of the chest, near the armpits and in the same vertical plane as the nipples.

- Usually, the lowest position of the dumbbells is a depth similar to that used in the flat barbell bench press. Visualize a bar passing through both dumbbell handles: The lowest position of the dumbbells is where the imaginary bar would touch the chest at nipple level. Lifters performing this exercise with the dumbbells in a neutral position can lower them farther, if desired, because the torso does not obstruct the path of the dumbbells.

- Do not arch the low back to raise the chest.

- Keep the head, torso, hips, and feet in a five-point body-contact position.

Downward Movement: Spotter

- Keep the hands near—but not touching—the lifter's forearms near the wrists as the dumbbells descend.

- Slightly flex the torso (but keep the back neutral) when following the path of the dumbbells.

Upward Movement: Lifter

▶ Press the dumbbells upward at the same rate and slightly toward each other to keep them under control.

▶ Maintain the same stationary five-point body-contact position; do not lift the head or arch the low back, and do not lift the buttocks or feet.

▶ Keep the wrists stiff, the forearms perpendicular to the floor, and the dumbbell handles in line with each other; do not allow the dumbbells to sway as they are pressed.

▶ Continue pressing the dumbbells up until the elbows are fully extended. Keep the forearms nearly parallel to each other; the dumbbells can move toward each other over the chest, but do not clang them together.

▶ At the completion of the set, first slowly lower the dumbbells to the chest (armpit) area and then, one at a time, return the dumbbells to the floor in a controlled manner.

Upward Movement: Spotter

▶ Keep the hands near—but not touching—the lifter's forearms near the wrists as the dumbbells ascend.

▶ Slightly extend the torso (but keep the back neutral) when following the path of the dumbbells.

3.4 INCLINE DUMBBELL BENCH PRESS

Video 3.4

Starting Position: Lifter

- Before picking up the dumbbells, check the seat of the incline bench. If it is adjustable, move the seat to allow for the following conditions:
  - The thighs are approximately parallel to the floor (with the feet flat).
  - The body is low enough so that the head is at the top of the bench.
  - The dumbbells will not hit the uprights of any of the racks (if they are present) during the exercise.
- Grasp two dumbbells of equal weight with a closed grip. Position the outside surface of the bottom half of the dumbbells against the front of the thighs (the dumbbell handles are parallel to each other).
- Sit on the seat of an incline bench with the dumbbells resting on the thighs.
- Lean back to place the head at the top of the bench. Once the inclined position is achieved, first move the dumbbells to the chest (armpit) area and then signal the spotter for assistance in moving them to a position above the neck and face with the elbows extended and arms parallel to each other.

  Reposition the head, shoulders, buttocks, and feet to achieve a five-point body-contact position:
  1. The head is placed firmly against the bench.
  2. The shoulders and upper back are placed firmly and evenly against the bench.
  3. The buttocks are placed evenly on the seat.
  4. The right foot is flat on the floor.
  5. The left foot is flat on the floor.
- The most common dumbbell position is with the dumbbell handles in line with each other with the palms facing toward the feet. Another option is to hold the dumbbells in a neutral position (i.e., parallel to each other with the palms facing each other).
- All repetitions begin from this extended-elbow position with the dumbbells supported over the neck and face.

Starting Position: Spotter

- Stand erect behind the head of the bench.
- Place the feet shoulder-width apart with the knees slightly flexed.
- Grasp the lifter's forearms near the wrists.
- At the lifter's signal, assist with moving the dumbbells to a position over the lifter's neck and face.
- Release the lifter's forearms smoothly.

Downward Movement: Lifter

▸ Begin the exercise by lowering the dumbbells slowly and under control toward the chest. To maintain a stable body position on the bench, lower the dumbbells at the same rate.

▸ Keep the wrists stiff, the forearms perpendicular to the floor, and the dumbbell handles in line with each other (unless using a neutral grip). Minimize all forward-to-backward and side-to-side movement.

▸ Guide the dumbbells down and slightly out to the lateral side of the chest, near the armpits and in line with the upper one-third of the chest (between the clavicles and the nipples).

▸ Usually, the lowest position of the dumbbells is a depth similar to that used in the incline barbell bench press. Visualize a bar passing through both dumbbell handles: The lowest position of the dumbbells is where the imaginary bar would touch the upper one-third of the chest. Lifters performing this exercise with the dumbbells in a neutral position can lower them farther, if desired, because the torso does not obstruct the path of the dumbbells.

INCLINE DUMBBELL BENCH PRESS

Starting positions   Downward and upward movements

- Do not arch the low back to raise the chest.
- Keep the head, torso, hips, and feet in a five-point body-contact position.

Downward Movement: Spotter

- Keep the hands near—but not touching—the lifter's forearms near the wrists as the dumbbells descend.
- Slightly flex the knees, hips, and torso, and keep the back neutral when following the path of the dumbbells.

Upward Movement: Lifter

- Press the dumbbells upward at the same rate and slightly toward each other to keep them under control. To keep them from falling forward (because of the angled torso position), press the dumbbells up over the shoulders (initially) and face (eventually) instead of out and away from the chest.
- Do not arch the low back, raise the hips, or push up with the legs (by trying to stand up). The body and feet should not move from their initial positions.
- Keep the wrists stiff, the forearms perpendicular to the floor, and the dumbbell handles in line with each other. Do not allow the dumbbells to sway as they are pressed.
- Continue pressing the dumbbells up until the elbows are fully extended. Keep the forearms nearly parallel to each other. The dumbbells can move toward each other over the chest, but do not clang them together.
- At the completion of the set, first slowly lower the dumbbells to the chest (armpit) area and then to the thighs; then, one at a time, return the dumbbells to the floor in a controlled manner.

Upward Movement: Spotter

- Keep the hands near—but not touching—the lifter's forearms near the wrists as the dumbbells ascend.
- Slightly extend the knees, hips, and torso, and keep the back neutral when following the path of the dumbbells.

UPPER BODY

3.5   VERTICAL CHEST PRESS (MACHINE)

Video 3.5

Starting Position

▸ Before performing this exercise, check the height of the seat and adjust it to allow for the following conditions:

- The thighs are approximately parallel to the floor (with the feet flat).
- The body is in line with the handgrips (an imaginary line connecting both handgrips should cross the front of the chest at nipple height).
- The arms are positioned approximately parallel to the floor when the elbows are extended and holding the handgrips (take the pin out of the weight stack, sit in the machine, and push the handles forward to check the arm position at a certain seat height).

▸ Sit on the seat and place the body in a five-point body-contact position:

1. The head is placed firmly against the vertical back pad.
2. The shoulders and upper back are placed firmly and evenly against the vertical back pad.

Starting position   Forward and backward movements

3. The buttocks are placed evenly on the seat.

4. The right foot is flat on the floor.

5. The left foot is flat on the floor.

- Grasp the handles with a closed, pronated (or neutral, if desired) grip.

- If the machine has a foot pedal, do the following:

  1. Use one foot to depress the pedal to move the handles forward.

  2. Grasp the handles.

  3. Slowly release the foot pedal and place the foot on the floor.

- If there is no foot pedal, grasp the handles one at a time and reposition the body in a five-point body-contact position.

- All repetitions begin from this position.

Forward Movement

- Begin the exercise by pushing the handles forward.

- Maintain the same stationary five-point body-contact position; do not arch the low back, lift the buttocks or feet, lift the head off of the pad, or contract the abdominals (to flex the torso forward).

- Keep the wrists stiff and continue pushing the handles until the elbows are fully extended but not forcefully locked.

Backward Movement

- Allow the handles to move toward the body slowly and under control.

- Keep the wrists stiff; the arms will be approximately parallel to the floor if the seat was adjusted properly before beginning the exercise.

- Guide the handles back to the chest; do not allow the handles to move backward rapidly to add a bounce to help with the next repetition.

- Keep the head, torso, hips, and feet in a five-point body-contact position.

- At the completion of the set, reverse the foot pedal procedure or guide the handles backward to their resting position by releasing the grip on one handle at a time.

Chest (Single-Joint) Exercises

Name	Description of the concentric action	PREDOMINANT MUSCLES INVOLVED	
		Muscle group or body area	Muscles
Pec deck (machine)	Shoulder transverse (horizontal) adduction	Chest	Pectoralis major
		Shoulders	Anterior deltoid
	Scapular protraction (abduction)	Scapulae	Serratus anterior
		Chest	Pectoralis minor
Flat dumbbell fly	Same as the pec deck (machine)		
Cable crossover (machine)	Same as the pec deck (machine)		

The icon denotes an exercise that requires a spotter.

3.6 PEC DECK (MACHINE)

Video 3.6

Starting Position

- Sit on the seat and place the body in a five-point body-contact position:

  1. The head is placed firmly against the vertical back pad (if the back pad is long enough).
  2. The shoulders and upper back are placed firmly and evenly against the vertical back pad.
  3. The buttocks are placed evenly on the seat.
  4. The right foot is flat on the floor.
  5. The left foot is flat on the floor.

- Grasp the handles one at a time with a closed, neutral grip with the elbows slightly flexed.

- Position the upper arms, elbows, and forearms parallel to the floor with the hands even with or slightly ahead of the front surface of the shoulders or chest.

- All repetitions begin from this position.

Starting position

Forward and backward movements

Forward Movement

- Begin the exercise by moving the handles toward each other at the same rate in a wide arc.
- Maintain the same stationary five-point body-contact position; do not arch the low back, lift the buttocks or feet, flex the torso forward, or jerk the torso or head forward.
- Keep the wrists stiff and the upper arms, elbows, and forearms parallel to the floor.
- Continue moving the handles toward each other until they meet in front of the face (or as far as they will move forward).

Backward Movement

- Allow the handles to swing out and back slowly and under control.
- Keep the wrists stiff and the upper arms, elbows, and forearms parallel to the floor.
- Guide the handles back to be in line with the chest and each other; do not rapidly swing the handles back to add momentum to help with the next repetition.
- Keep the head, torso, hips, and feet in a five-point body-contact position.
- At the completion of the set, guide the handles backward by slightly twisting the body to each side to return each handle, one at a time, to its resting position.

3.7 FLAT DUMBBELL FLY

Video 3.7

Starting Position: Lifter

▶ Grasp two dumbbells of equal weight with a closed grip. Position the outside surface of the bottom half of the dumbbells against the front of the thighs (the dumbbell handles will be parallel to each other).

▶ Sit on one end of a flat bench with the dumbbells resting on the thighs.

▶ Lie back so the head rests on the other end of the bench. Once the supine position is achieved, first move the dumbbells to the chest (armpit) area and then signal the spotter for assistance in moving them to a position above the chest with the elbows extended and forearms parallel to each other.

▶ Reposition the head, shoulders, buttocks, and feet to achieve a five-point body-contact position:

1. The head is placed firmly on the bench.
2. The shoulders and upper back are placed firmly and evenly on the bench.
3. The buttocks are placed evenly on the bench.
4. The right foot is flat on the floor.
5. The left foot is flat on the floor.

Starting positions

Downward movement positions

UPPER BODY

- The dumbbells should be in a neutral hand position with the handles parallel to each other and the elbows pointing out to the sides.

- Slightly flex the elbows and hold this flexed position throughout the exercise.

- All repetitions begin with the arms in this position with the dumbbells supported over the chest.

Starting Position: Spotter

- Get into a low (but still erect) body position close to the head of the bench.

- To create a stable spotting position, get into a fully lunged position with one knee on the floor and the foot of the other leg ahead of the rear knee and flat on the floor.

- Grasp the lifter's forearms near the wrists.

- At the lifter's signal, assist with moving the dumbbells to a position over the lifter's chest.

- Release the lifter's forearms smoothly.

Downward Movement: Lifter

- Begin the exercise by lowering the dumbbells slowly in wide arcs under control. No movement should occur at the elbow joints; movement should occur only at the shoulders. To maintain a stable body position on the bench, lower the dumbbells at the same rate.

- Keep the wrists stiff and the elbows locked in a slightly flexed position with the dumbbell handles parallel to each other throughout the movement.

- The hands, wrists, forearms, elbows, upper arms, and shoulders should stay nearly in the same vertical plane.

- The elbows should transition from pointing out to the sides to pointing toward the floor during the downward movement.

- Continue to lower the dumbbells in wide arcs until they are level with the top of the chest.

- Keep the head, torso, hips, and feet in a five-point body-contact position.

Downward Movement: Spotter

- Keep the hands near—but not touching—the lifter's forearms near the wrists as the dumbbells descend.

- Slightly flex the torso (but keep the back neutral) when following the path of the dumbbells.

Upward Movement: Lifter

- Raise the dumbbells upward in wide arcs under control; imagine hugging a large tree trunk with the arms.

- Keep the wrists stiff and the elbows locked in a slightly flexed position.

▶ Maintain the same stationary five-point body-contact position; do not arch the low back, lift the buttocks or feet, lift the head, or shrug the shoulders to help raise the dumbbells.

▶ The hands, wrists, forearms, elbows, upper arms, and shoulders should stay in nearly the same vertical plane during the upward movement.

▶ Continue raising the dumbbells until they are positioned over the chest in the starting position.

▶ At the completion of the set, first slowly lower the dumbbells to the chest (armpit) area and then, one at a time, return the dumbbells to the floor in a controlled manner.

Upward Movement: Spotter

▶ Keep the hands near—but not touching—the lifter's forearms near the wrists as the dumbbells ascend.

▶ Slightly extend the torso (but keep the back neutral) when following the path of the dumbbells.

3.8 CABLE CROSSOVER (MACHINE)

Video 3.8

Starting Position

- ▸ Before performing this exercise, check that the same weight is selected for both weight stacks.

- ▸ Stand near a weight stack (with the weight stacks behind the body) and reach back with the left (or right) hand to grasp the handle with a closed, neutral grip. Pull the handle down and toward the left (or right) side of the body.

- ▸ Move toward the other weight stack and grasp the other handle with the right (or left) hand with a closed, neutral grip. Pull the handle down and toward the right (or left) side of the body.

- ▸ Move to a position on the floor between the two weight stacks.

- ▸ Slightly flex the elbows, take a step forward with one foot (to get into a staggered stance with the lead knee moderately flexed and the trailing knee fully extended) while allowing the shoulders to horizontally abduct (or diagonally abduct, depending on the height of the machine relative to the shoulders) away from and behind the torso. The cables should be taut in this position.

- ▸ Keeping the head in line with the spine, slightly flex the torso and check that the feet are pointing straight ahead.

Starting position   Forward and backward movements

▲ Check that the elbows are slightly flexed and the handles are held with a neutral grip; these positions are held throughout the exercise.

▲ All repetitions begin from this position.

Forward Movement

▲ Begin the exercise by adducting the shoulders in wide arcs under control. No movement should occur at the elbow joints; movement should occur only at the shoulders. To maintain a stable body position, move the handles toward each other at the same rate.

▲ Maintain the same slightly forward-flexed torso position. Keep the wrists stiff and the elbows locked in a slightly flexed position with the handles nearly parallel to each other throughout the movement.

▲ Continue to adduct the shoulders until the handles are brought together in front of the chest.

Backward Movement

▲ Allow the handles to swing out slowly and under control back to the starting position.

▲ Maintain the same slightly forward-flexed torso position. Keep the wrists stiff and the elbows locked in a slightly flexed position with the handles nearly parallel to each other.

▲ At the completion of the set, take a step back and toward one of the weight stacks and guide the handle toward the machine to slowly return the weight stack to a resting position. Then, take a step toward the other weight stack and guide the handle toward the machine to slowly return the remaining weight stack to a resting position.

Back (Multijoint) Exercises

Name	Description of the concentric action	PREDOMINANT MUSCLES INVOLVED	
		Muscle group or body area	Muscles
Lat pulldown (machine)	Shoulder adduction	Upper back	Latissimus dorsi
			Teres major
	Scapular retraction and depression (adduction)	Upper back, midback	Middle trapezius
			Lower trapezius
			Rhomboids
	Shoulder extension	Back	Latissimus dorsi
			Teres major
		Shoulders	Posterior deltoid
	Elbow flexion	Upper arm (anterior)	Brachialis
			Biceps brachii
			Brachioradialis
Bent-over row	Same as the lat pulldown (machine), but the concentric action does not include shoulder adduction		
One-arm dumbbell row	Same as the lat pulldown (machine), but the concentric action does not include shoulder adduction		
Low-pulley seated row (machine)	Same as the lat pulldown (machine), but the concentric action does not include shoulder adduction		
Seated row (machine)	Same as the lat pulldown (machine), but the concentric action does not include shoulder adduction		
Face pull (machine)	Scapular retraction	Upper back, midback	Latissimus dorsi
			Teres major
			Middle trapezius
			Rhomboids

UPPER BODY

3.9 LAT PULLDOWN (MACHINE)

Video 3.9

Starting Position

▸ Grasp the long bar with a closed, pronated grip (various bar attachments can be used for this exercise; most are 36 to 48 inches [91 to 122 cm] long with slightly angled ends).

▸ A common grip width using the long bar involves placing the index finger on the outside bends of the bar. If the bar is entirely straight, then use a grip that is wider than shoulder-width and spaced evenly on the bar.

▸ Pull the bar down and move into one of the following positions:

- If a seat is attached to the machine, sit down facing the weight stack with the legs under the thigh pads and the feet flat on the floor, if possible (if the bench seat is adjustable, position the thighs approximately parallel to the floor with the feet flat on the floor).

- If there is no seat attached to the machine, kneel on one knee facing the machine and under the top pulley. The foot of the other leg is placed ahead of the body, flat on the floor.

Starting position | Downward and upward movements

- The elbows should be fully extended with the selected load suspended above the remainder of the weight stack.

- Before beginning the exercise, lean the torso slightly backward and extend the neck to create a clear path for the bar to pass by the face as it is pulled down. This position will also reduce impingement stress on the shoulder joints. All repetitions begin from this position.

Downward Movement

- Begin the exercise by pulling down on the bar; the elbows should move down and back and the chest up and out as the bar is lowered.

- Maintain the same stationary body position; do not jerk the torso or lean back quickly to help pull the bar down.

- Continue pulling the bar down and toward the body (not just down) until it lightly touches the clavicle and upper chest area. The torso should still have a slight backward lean at the bottom bar position.

Upward Movement

- Guide the bar slowly and under control back up to the starting position; do not allow the bar to jerk the arms upward.

- Maintain the same backward torso lean and lower body position.

- The elbows should be fully extended at the end of the upward movement.

- At the completion of the set, stand up slowly and guide the bar under control to its resting position.

UPPER BODY

3.10   BENT-OVER ROW

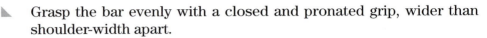

Starting Position

▸ Grasp the bar evenly with a closed and pronated grip, wider than shoulder-width apart.

▸ Follow the preparatory body position and lifting guidelines to lift the bar off the floor to a position at the front of the thighs. The body should be fully erect before moving into the flexed torso position of the bent-over row.

▸ Place the feet shoulder-width apart (or slightly wider) with the knees slightly flexed.

▸ Flex forward at the hips so the torso is nearly parallel to the floor while maintaining the same flexed knee position.

▸ Pull the shoulders back, push the chest out, and extend the neck slightly to create a neutral or slightly concave (not rounded) back position. Do not attempt to look up at the ceiling; just focus on the floor a short distance ahead of the feet.

▸ Allow the bar to hang at full elbow extension; adjust the amount of knee and torso flexion so the weight plates are not touching the floor. All repetitions begin from this position.

Starting position   Upward and downward movements

Upward Movement

- Begin the exercise by pulling the bar up toward the torso; the elbows should point out to the sides, away from the body, with the wrists kept straight. Do not curl the bar upward.

- Maintain the same stationary body position; do not shrug the shoulders, swing the body (i.e., extend the spine), hyperextend the neck, extend the knees, or rise up on the toes to help raise the bar upward.

- Continue pulling the bar up until it touches the sternum or upper abdomen. At the highest bar position, the elbows will be higher than the torso (when seen from the side).

Downward Movement

- Lower the bar slowly and under control to the starting position; do not flex the torso forward, extend the knees, or allow the body's weight to shift toward the toes.

- Maintain the same stationary torso, neutral spine, and flexed knee positions with the feet flat on the floor.

- The elbows should be fully extended at the end of the downward movement.

- At the completion of the set, slowly flex the hips and knees at the same rate to squat down and return the bar to the floor in a controlled manner.

3.11   ONE-ARM DUMBBELL ROW

Starting Position

▶ Stand on the side of a flat bench (with the body perpendicular, not parallel, to the length of the bench) with a dumbbell on the floor.

▶ Position the feet shoulder-width apart and slightly flex the knees.

▶ Reach down with one hand and grasp the dumbbell with a closed, neutral grip.

▶ Flex forward at the hips so the torso is slightly above parallel to the floor with the dumbbell hanging down at full elbow extension. The opposite hand should be placed on the bench for support.

▶ Pull the shoulders back, push the chest out, and slightly extend the neck to create a neutral spine position. Do not attempt to look up at the ceiling; just focus on the floor a short distance ahead of the feet.

▶ All repetitions begin from this position.

Upward Movement

▶ Begin the exercise by pulling the dumbbell up toward the torso; the upper arm and elbow should be kept near the side of the body with the wrist straight. Do not curl the dumbbell upward or inward.

Starting position

Upward and downward movements

- Maintain the same stationary body position; do not swing or jerk the upper body upward to help raise the dumbbell.

- Continue pulling the dumbbell up until it touches the side of the outer chest or rib cage area. At the highest dumbbell position, the elbow will be higher than the torso (when seen from the side).

Downward Movement

- Lower the dumbbell slowly and under control to the starting position; do not allow the dumbbell to jerk the arm down.

- Maintain the same stationary torso, neutral spine, and flexed knee positions with both feet flat on the floor.

- After completing a set with one arm, repeat the procedure using the other arm.

3.12 LOW-PULLEY SEATED ROW (MACHINE)

Starting Position

- Sit on the long seat pad (or if one is not present, sit on the floor) facing the machine.

- Place the feet on the foot supports or the machine frame.

- Flex the knees and hips to reach forward and grasp the handles with a closed, neutral grip (various attachments can be used for this exercise; one of the most common is a triangular-shaped double handle that places the hands in a neutral grip; however, a pronated grip can be used as well).

- Pull the handles back and sit in an erect seated position with the torso perpendicular to the floor, knees slightly flexed, and the feet and legs parallel to each other.

- The elbows should be fully extended and the arms parallel to the floor (or slightly below) with the selected load suspended above the remainder of the weight stack. All repetitions begin from this position.

Starting position

Backward and forward movements

Backward Movement

▸ Begin the exercise by pulling the handles toward the abdomen. The elbows should stay relatively near or next to the sides of the torso, not pointing directly out to the sides.

▸ Maintain the same stationary body position; do not jerk the torso, extend the knees, or quickly lean back to help pull the handles.

▸ Continue pulling the handles until the forearms or wrists press against the torso, or until the handles (or bar, depending on what attachment is used) touch the abdomen.

Forward Movement

▸ Guide the handles slowly and under control back to the starting position; do not allow the handles to jerk the arms forward.

▸ Maintain the same stationary torso and flexed knee positions.

▸ The elbows should be fully extended at the end of the forward movement.

▸ At the completion of the set, slowly flex the knees and hips to move forward and return the handles to the resting position.

3.13 SEATED ROW (MACHINE)

Video 3.13

Starting Position

▸ Before performing this exercise, check the height of the seat and position of the chest pad and adjust them to allow for the following conditions:

- The thighs are approximately parallel to the floor (with the feet flat or on the foot supports).
- The torso is perpendicular to the floor when sitting erect with the torso against the chest pad.
- The arms are approximately parallel to the floor when holding the handles.

▸ Sit erect with the feet flat on the floor or on the foot supports, and press the torso against the chest pad.

▸ Grasp the handles with a closed, pronated grip (or neutral grip, if desired), and then reposition the body to achieve the seated erect torso position.

Starting position

Backward and forward movements

- The elbows should be fully extended and the arms approximately parallel to the floor with the selected load suspended above the remainder of the weight stack. All repetitions begin from this position.

Backward Movement

- Begin the exercise by pulling the handles toward the torso, chest, upper abdomen, or lower abdomen, depending on the type of machine. The elbows should stay relatively near or next to the sides of the torso (depending on what handle is used), not pointing directly out to the sides.

- Maintain the same stationary body position; do not lean back quickly to help pull the handles.

- Continue pulling the handles until the forearms or wrists press against the torso or until the handles touch the torso.

Forward Movement

- Allow the handles to move slowly and under control to the starting position; do not allow the handles to jerk the arms forward.

- Maintain the same stationary torso position.

- The elbows should be fully extended at the end of the forward movement.

- At the completion of the set, guide the handles back to the resting position.

UPPER BODY

3.14   FACE PULL (MACHINE)

Video 3.14

Starting Position

▶ Stand facing a high-pulley cable machine and grasp a rope handle with a closed, pronated grip and the palms facing the floor.

▶ Step back far enough from the machine so there is tension on the cable when the arms are fully extended in front of the face with the elbows pointing out to the sides. Use a parallel foot stance with flexed knees to create a stable body position.

▶ Check that the head is in line with the spine and the torso is fully erect.

▶ All repetitions begin from this position.

Backward Movement

▶ Begin the exercise by first retracting the scapulae with the elbows still fully extended.

▶ Pull the handle toward the face by horizontally abducting the shoulders and flexing the elbows.

Starting position   Backward and forward movements

▶ When the upper arms become aligned with the frontal plane at the shoulders, externally rotate the upper arms and continue the backward movement until the center clasp of the handle comes close to the face.

Forward Movement

▶ Allow the upper arms to internally rotate, the elbows to extend, the shoulders to horizontally adduct, and the scapulae to protract back to the starting position.

▶ Maintain the same head, torso, and body position throughout the movement.

▶ At the completion of the set, move forward to return the weight stack to a resting position.

Shoulder (Multijoint) Exercises

Name	Description of the concentric action	PREDOMINANT MUSCLES INVOLVED	
		Muscle group or body area	Muscles
Shoulder press (machine)	Shoulder abduction	Shoulders	Anterior deltoids
			Medial deltoids
	Scapular protraction (abduction)	Upper shoulders and upper back	Trapezius
		Scapulae	Serratus anterior
	Elbow extension	Upper arm (posterior)	Triceps brachii
Seated barbell shoulder press	Same as the shoulder press (machine)		
Seated dumbbell shoulder press	Same as the shoulder press (machine)		
Upright row	Shoulder abduction	Shoulders	Anterior deltoids
			Medial deltoids
			Posterior deltoids
	Scapular elevation	Shoulders and upper back	Trapezius
		Scapulae	Serratus anterior
	Elbow flexion	Upper arm (anterior)	Brachialis
			Biceps brachii
			Brachioradialis

The icon denotes an exercise that requires a spotter.

3.15 SHOULDER PRESS (MACHINE)

Video 3.15

Starting Position

▸ Before performing this exercise, check the height of the seat and adjust it to allow for the following conditions:

- The thighs are parallel to the floor (with the feet flat).
- The shoulders are approximately in line with the handgrips (an imaginary line connecting both handgrips should not cross lower than the top of the shoulders or the base of the neck).
- The body is low enough that the head is in contact with the pad at the top of the bench.

▸ Sit on the seat and lean back to place the body in a five-point body-contact position:

1. The head is placed firmly against the vertical back pad.
2. The shoulders and upper back are placed firmly and evenly against the vertical back pad.

Starting position

Upward and downward movements

3. The buttocks are placed evenly on the seat.

4. The right foot is flat on the floor.

5. The left foot is flat on the floor.

▶ Grasp the handles with a closed, pronated grip (or neutral grip, if desired). All repetitions begin from this position.

Upward Movement

▶ Begin the exercise by pressing the handles upward.

▶ Maintain the same stationary five-point body-contact position; do not arch the low back, raise the buttocks, or push upward with the legs.

▶ Keep the wrists stiff and the forearms approximately parallel to each other; continue pressing the handles until the elbows are fully extended but not forcefully locked.

Downward Movement

▶ Allow the handles to move slowly and under control back to the starting position; do not flex the torso forward as the handles are lowered.

▶ Maintain the same stationary five-point body-contact position; do not allow the handles to move downward rapidly to add a bounce to help with the next repetition.

At the completion of the set, return the handles to the resting position.

3.16   SEATED BARBELL SHOULDER PRESS

Video 3.16

Starting Position: Lifter

▶ Before performing this exercise, check the seat of the shoulder press bench. If it is adjustable, move the seat to allow for the following conditions:

- The thighs are approximately parallel to the floor (with the feet flat).

- The head is lower than the racked bar and resting at the top of the bench (if the bench has a long vertical back pad).

- The bar can be lifted off and returned to the supporting pins or ledge without hitting the top of the head (the seat is too high) or requiring the use of the legs to help reach the rack (the seat is too low).

▶ Sit on the seat in a five-point body-contact position:

1. The head is placed firmly against the vertical back pad (if the back pad is long enough).

2. The shoulders and upper back are placed firmly and evenly against the vertical back pad.

Starting positions

Downward and upward movements

UPPER BODY

3. The buttocks are placed evenly on the seat.

4. The right foot is flat on the floor.

5. The left foot is flat on the floor.

▸ Grasp the bar evenly with a closed and pronated grip, slightly wider than shoulder-width apart.

▸ Signal the spotter for assistance to move the bar off the rack to a position over the head with the elbows fully extended. This is the liftoff. All repetitions begin from this position.

Starting Position: Spotter

▸ Stand erect behind the back of the bench.

▸ Place the feet shoulder-width apart with the knees slightly flexed.

▸ Grasp the bar with a closed, alternated grip inside the lifter's hands.

▸ At the lifter's signal, assist with moving the bar off the rack.

▸ Guide the bar to a position over the lifter's head.

▸ Release the bar smoothly.

Downward Movement: Lifter

▸ Begin the exercise by lowering the bar slowly and under control.

▸ Keep the wrists stiff and the forearms perpendicular to the floor and parallel to each other. The width of the grip will determine how parallel the forearms are to each other.

▸ Extend the neck slightly to lower the bar directly in front of the face; do not let the bar hit the forehead or nose as it is lowered.

▸ Continue to lower the bar until it lightly touches the clavicles; do not bounce the bar on the shoulders or arch the low back.

▸ Keep the head, torso, hips, and feet in a five-point body-contact position.

Downward Movement: Spotter

▸ Keep the hands in the alternated grip position close to—but not touching—the bar as it descends.

▸ Slightly flex the knees, hips, and torso, and keep the back neutral when following the path of the bar.

Upward Movement: Lifter

▸ Extend the neck slightly to press the bar straight upward until it passes by the forehead.

▸ Do not arch the low back, raise the hips, or push up with the legs (by trying to stand up); the body and feet should not move from their initial positions.

▸ Keep the wrists stiff and the forearms perpendicular to the floor and parallel to each other.

▸ Continue pressing the bar up until the elbows are fully extended (but not forcefully locked) with the bar overhead.

▸ At the completion of the set, signal the spotter for assistance to rack the bar, but keep a grip on the bar until both ends are secure and motionless on the supporting pins or ledge.

Upward Movement: Spotter

▸ Keep the hands in the alternated grip position close to—but not touching—the bar as it ascends.

▸ Slightly extend the knees, hips, and torso, and keep the back neutral when following the path of the bar.

▸ At the lifter's signal after the set is completed, grasp the bar with an alternated grip inside the lifter's hands.

▸ Guide the bar back onto the rack.

▸ Keep a grip on the bar until it is secure and motionless on the supporting pins or ledge.

3.17 SEATED DUMBBELL SHOULDER PRESS

 Video 3.17

Starting Position: Lifter

▶ Before picking up the dumbbells, check the seat of the bench. If it is adjustable, move the seat to allow for the following conditions:

- The thighs are approximately parallel to the floor (with the feet flat).
- The body is low enough so that the head is at the top of the bench (if the bench has a long vertical back pad).
- The dumbbells will not hit the uprights of any of the racks (if they are present) during the exercise.

▶ Grasp two equal-weight dumbbells with a closed grip. Position the outside surface of the bottom half of the dumbbells against the front of the thighs (the dumbbell handles will be parallel to each other).

▶ Sit on the seat with the dumbbells resting on the thighs. Move the dumbbells to the outside of the shoulders so that the dumbbell handles are level with the top of the shoulders or the base of the neck.

▶ Reposition the head, shoulders, buttocks, and feet to achieve a five-point body-contact position:

1. The head is placed firmly against the vertical back pad (if the back pad is long enough; the photos show a short vertical back pad).
2. The shoulders and upper back are placed firmly and evenly against the vertical back pad.
3. The buttocks are placed evenly on the seat.
4. The right foot is flat on the floor.
5. The left foot is flat on the floor.

▶ The most common dumbbell position is with the dumbbell handles in line with each other with the palms facing away from the face. Another option is to hold the dumbbells in a neutral position (i.e., parallel to each other with the palms facing each other).

▶ All repetitions begin from this position.

Starting Position: Spotter

▶ Stand erect behind the back of the bench.
▶ Place the feet shoulder-width apart with the knees slightly flexed.
▶ Grasp the lifter's forearms near the wrists.
▶ At the lifter's signal, assist with moving the dumbbells to a position outside the shoulders.
▶ Release the lifter's forearms smoothly.

Upward Movement: Lifter

▶ Begin the exercise by pressing the dumbbells upward at the same rate and slightly toward each other to keep them under control.

- Maintain the same stationary five-point body-contact position; do not arch the low back, raise the buttocks, or push upward with the legs.
- Keep the wrists stiff, the forearms perpendicular to the floor, and the dumbbell handles in line with each other; do not allow the dumbbells to sway as they are pressed.
- The hands, elbows, and shoulders should be in the same vertical plane.
- Continue pressing the dumbbells up until the elbows are fully extended. Keep the forearms nearly parallel to each other; the dumbbells can move toward each other over the head, but do not clang them together.

Upward Movement: Spotter

- Keep the hands near—but not touching—the lifter's forearms near the wrists as the dumbbells ascend.

SEATED DUMBBELL SHOULDER PRESS

Starting positions   Upward and downward movements

▶ Slightly extend the knees, hips, and torso, and keep the back neutral when following the path of the dumbbells.

Downward Movement: Lifter

▶ Lower the dumbbells slowly and under control to the starting position. To maintain a stable body position on the bench, lower the dumbbells at the same rate.

▶ Keep the wrists stiff, the forearms perpendicular to the floor, and the dumbbell handles in line with each other.

▶ Continue to lower the dumbbells until they are level with the top of the shoulders or the base of the neck; do not bounce the dumbbells on the shoulders or shrug the shoulders to meet the dumbbells.

▶ Keep the head, torso, hips, and feet in a five-point body-contact position.

▶ At the completion of the set, slowly lower the dumbbells to the thighs; then, one at a time, return the dumbbells to the floor in a controlled manner.

Downward Movement: Spotter

▶ Keep the hands near—but not touching—the lifter's forearms near the wrists as the dumbbells descend.

▶ Slightly flex the knees, hips, and torso, and keep the back neutral when following the path of the dumbbells.

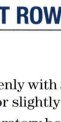

Video 3.18

3.18 UPRIGHT ROW

Starting Position

- Grasp the bar evenly with a closed and pronated grip, approximately shoulder-width or slightly wider apart.

- Follow the preparatory body position and lifting guidelines to lift the bar off the floor to a position at the front of the thighs.

- Place the feet shoulder- or hip-width apart with the knees slightly flexed, torso erect, shoulders held back, and eyes focused ahead.

- Allow the bar to hang at full elbow extension. All repetitions begin from this position.

Upward Movement

- Begin the exercise by pulling the bar up along the abdomen and chest by abducting the shoulders and flexing the elbows.

- Keep the elbows pointed out to the sides as the bar brushes against the body; do not curl the bar upward.

- Maintain the same stationary body position; do not shrug the shoulders, swing the body (i.e., hyperextend the spine), hyperextend the neck, extend the knees, or rise up on the toes to help raise the bar upward.

Starting position

Upward and downward movements

UPPER BODY

▰ Continue pulling the bar up until it reaches the area between the bottom of the sternum and the chin (depending on arm length and shoulder flexibility). At the highest bar position, the elbows should be level with or slightly higher than the shoulders and wrists.

Downward Movement

▰ Lower the bar slowly and under control to the starting position; do not flex the torso forward, bounce the bar on the thighs at the bottom position, or allow the body's weight to shift toward the toes.

▰ Maintain the same stationary body position with the feet flat on the floor.

▰ The elbows should be fully extended at the end of the downward movement.

▰ At the completion of the set, slowly flex the hips and knees at the same rate (to keep an erect torso position) to squat down and return the bar to the floor in a controlled manner.

Shoulder (Single-Joint) Exercises

Name	Description of the concentric action	PREDOMINANT MUSCLES INVOLVED	
		Muscle group or body area	Muscles
Lateral shoulder raise	Shoulder abduction	Shoulders	Medial deltoid
Bent-over lateral raise	Shoulder transverse (horizontal) abduction	Shoulders	Posterior deltoid

UPPER BODY

3.19 LATERAL SHOULDER RAISE

Video 3.19

Starting Position

- ▸ Grasp two dumbbells of equal weight with a closed, neutral grip.
- ▸ Follow the preparatory body position and lifting guidelines to lift the dumbbells off the floor to a position hanging next to the thighs.
- ▸ Place the feet shoulder- or hip-width apart with the knees slightly flexed, torso erect, shoulders held back, and eyes focused ahead.
- ▸ Move the dumbbells to the front of the thighs and position them with the palms facing each other (this creates a neutral grip position).
- ▸ Slightly flex the elbows and hold this flexed position throughout the exercise. (*Note:* The elbows should be slightly more flexed than what is seen in the photos and the video clip.) All repetitions begin from this position.

Upward Movement

- ▸ Begin the exercise by raising the dumbbells up and out to the sides. No movement should occur at the elbow joints; movement should occur only at the shoulders.

Starting position

Upward and downward movements

- Keep the wrists stiff and the elbows locked in a slightly flexed position; maintain a neutral grip on the dumbbells.
- The upper arms and elbows should rise together ahead of the forearms, hands, and dumbbells.
- Maintain the same stationary body position; do not shrug the shoulders, swing the body (i.e., hyperextend the spine), extend the knees, or rise up on the toes to help raise the dumbbells.
- Continue raising the dumbbells until the arms are parallel to the floor or approximately level with the shoulders.

Downward Movement

- Lower the dumbbells slowly and under control to the starting position; do not flex the torso forward, extend the knees, or allow the body's weight to shift toward the toes.
- Keep the wrists stiff and the elbows locked in a slightly flexed position.
- Maintain the same stationary body position; do not allow the dumbbells to jerk the arms down.
- Continue to lower the dumbbells until they return to the front of the thighs; do not bounce the dumbbells on the thighs to help with the next repetition.
- At the completion of the set, slowly flex the hips and knees at the same rate (to keep an erect torso position) to squat down and return the dumbbells to the floor in a controlled manner.

UPPER BODY

3.20   BENT-OVER LATERAL RAISE

Video 3.20

Starting Position

- Grasp two equal-weight dumbbells with a closed grip.

- Follow the preparatory body position and lifting guidelines to lift the dumbbells off the floor to a position hanging next to the thighs. The body should be fully erect before moving into the flexed torso position of the bent-over lateral raise.

- Place the feet shoulder- or hip-width apart with the knees slightly flexed.

- Flex the torso forward to slightly above parallel to the floor while maintaining the same flexed knee position.

- Pull the shoulders back, push the chest out, and extend the neck slightly to create a neutral or slightly concave (not rounded) back position. Do not attempt to look up at the ceiling; just focus on the floor a short distance ahead of the feet.

- Allow the dumbbells to hang; adjust the amount of knee and torso flexion so the dumbbells are not touching the floor.

- Reposition the dumbbells in a neutral hand position with the handles parallel to each other and the elbows pointing out to the sides.

Starting position

Upward and downward movements

> Slightly flex the elbows and hold the flexed position throughout the exercise. (*Note:* The elbows should be slightly more flexed than what is seen in the photos and the video clip.) All repetitions begin from this position.

Upward Movement

> Begin the exercise by raising the dumbbells up and out to the sides. No movement should occur at the elbow joints; movement should occur only at the shoulders.

> Keep the wrists stiff and the elbows locked in a slightly flexed position; maintain a neutral grip on the dumbbells.

> The upper arms, elbows, forearms, and dumbbells should stay nearly in the same vertical plane (perpendicular to the body) during the upward movement. The elbows should rise together and ahead of and slightly higher than the dumbbells.

> Maintain the neutral spine, stationary torso, and flexed knee positions with the feet flat on the floor; do not swing the body (i.e., extend the spine), extend the knees, or rise up on the toes to help raise the dumbbells.

> Continue raising the dumbbells until the upper arms are approximately parallel to the floor or approximately level with the shoulders. At the highest position, the elbows will be slightly higher than the dumbbells (when seen from the side).

Downward Movement

> Lower the dumbbells slowly and under control to the starting position; do not flex the torso forward, extend the knees, or allow the body's weight to shift toward the toes.

> Keep the wrists stiff and the elbows locked in a slightly flexed position.

> Maintain the neutral spine, stationary torso, and flexed knee positions with the feet flat on the floor.

> Continue to lower the dumbbells until they return to their hanging starting position; keep the dumbbell handles parallel to each other during the downward movement.

> At the completion of the set, slowly flex the hips and knees at the same rate to squat down and return the dumbbells to the floor in a controlled manner.

Biceps (Single-Joint) Exercises

Name	Description of the concentric action	PREDOMINANT MUSCLES INVOLVED	
		Muscle group or body area	Muscles
Barbell biceps curl	Elbow flexion	Upper arm (anterior)	Brachialis
			Biceps brachii
			Brachioradialis
Hammer curl	Same as the barbell biceps curl		Brachialis
			Biceps brachii
			Brachioradialis

3.21   BARBELL BICEPS CURL

Video 3.21

This exercise commonly uses (but does not require) a *cambered* bar (sometimes also called an *EZ-curl* bar), which is a short bar that is bent to create two distinct hand placements: an inside and an outside grip. Holding the bar to form an *M* with the bends allows the hands to grasp the bar evenly with a narrow, inside grip. Reversing the bar to form a *W* with the bends results in a wide, outside grip. Either grip can be used.

Starting Position

- Grasp the bar evenly with a closed, supinated grip.

- Follow the preparatory body position and lifting guidelines to lift the bar off the floor to a position at the front of the thighs.

- A common grip width involves placing the hands on the bar so the arms touch the sides of the torso or hips; the nonthumb sides of the hands are next to (and in contact with) the sides of the thighs.

- Place the feet shoulder- or hip-width apart with the knees slightly flexed, torso erect, shoulders held back, and eyes focused ahead.

- Allow the bar to rest against the front of the thighs at full elbow extension. All repetitions begin from this position.

Starting position

Upward and downward movements

Upward Movement

- Begin the exercise by raising the bar in an arc by flexing the elbows.

- Keep the wrists stiff and the upper arms stationary against the sides of the torso as the bar is raised; do not let them move forward or outward. No movement should occur at the shoulders; movement should occur only at the elbow joints.

- Maintain the same stationary body position; do not swing the body (i.e., hyperextend the spine), shrug the shoulders, hyperextend the neck, extend the knees, or rise up on the toes to help raise the bar upward.

- Continue flexing the elbows until the bar is near the anterior deltoids. If the elbows move forward at the highest bar position, then the elbows have flexed too far.

Downward Movement

- Lower the bar slowly and under control to the starting position by extending the elbows; do not bounce the bar on the thighs at the bottom position, flex the torso forward, extend the knees, or allow the body's weight to shift toward the toes.

- Keep the wrists stiff and the upper arms stationary against the sides of the torso.

- Maintain the same stationary body position with the feet flat on the floor.

- Continue to lower the bar until the elbows are fully extended but not forcefully locked.

- At the completion of the set, slowly flex the hips and knees at the same rate (to keep an erect torso position) to squat down and return the bar to the floor in a controlled manner.

3.22   HAMMER CURL

Video 3.22

Starting Position

▸ Grasp two equal-weight dumbbells with a closed, neutral grip.

▸ Follow the preparatory body position and lifting guidelines to lift the dumbbells off the floor to a position hanging next to the thighs.

▸ A common arm position involves hanging the arms at the sides of the torso or hips with the palms facing the outer thighs.

▸ Place the feet shoulder- or hip-width apart with the knees slightly flexed, torso erect, shoulders held back, and eyes focused ahead.

▸ Allow the dumbbells to hang at full elbow extension. All repetitions begin from this position.

Upward Movement

▸ Begin the exercise by raising one dumbbell upward in an arc by flexing the elbow. The other arm should be kept stationary at the side of the thigh (only one arm is involved at a time).

Starting position

Upward and downward movements

- Keep the wrist stiff and the upper arm stationary against the side of the torso as the dumbbell is raised; do not let it move forward or outward. No movement should occur at the shoulder; movement should occur only at the elbow joint.

- The dumbbell should remain in a neutral position as it is raised.

- Maintain the same stationary body position; do not swing the body (i.e., hyperextend the spine), shrug the shoulders, hyperextend the neck, extend the knees, or rise up on the toes to help raise the dumbbell upward.

- Continue flexing the elbow until the top half of the dumbbell is near the anterior deltoid in a neutral hand position. If the elbow moves forward at the highest dumbbell position, then the elbow has flexed too far.

Downward Movement

- Lower the dumbbell slowly and under control to the starting position, maintaining a neutral grip.

- Do not flex the torso forward, extend the knees, or allow the body's weight to shift toward the toes.

- Keep the wrist stiff and the upper arm stationary against the side of the torso.

- Maintain the same stationary body position with the feet flat on the floor.

- Continue to lower the dumbbell until the elbow is fully extended but not forcefully locked.

- The other arm should be kept stationary at the side of the thigh.

- Repeat the upward and downward movements with the other arm; the arm just used should remain stationary until the dumbbell in the other hand returns to the starting position. Continue to alternate arms to complete the set.

- At the completion of the set, slowly flex the hips and knees at the same rate (to keep an erect torso position) to squat down and return the dumbbells to the floor in a controlled manner.

Triceps (Single-Joint) Exercises

Name	Description of the concentric action	PREDOMINANT MUSCLES INVOLVED	
		Muscle group or body area	Muscles
Lying barbell triceps extension	Elbow extension	Upper arm (posterior)	Triceps brachii
Triceps pushdown (machine)	Same as the lying barbell triceps extension		

The icon denotes an exercise that requires a spotter.

3.23 LYING BARBELL TRICEPS EXTENSION

Video 3.23

Starting Position: Lifter

▸ Sit on one end of a flat bench and then lie back so the head rests on the other end of the bench.

▸ Position the head, shoulders, buttocks, and feet to achieve a five-point body-contact position:

1. The head is placed firmly on the bench.
2. The shoulders and upper back are placed firmly and evenly on the bench.
3. The buttocks are placed evenly on the bench.
4. The right foot is flat on the floor.
5. The left foot is flat on the floor.

▸ Signal the spotter to pick up the bar off the floor.

▸ Grasp the bar with a closed, pronated grip.

▸ Move the bar to a position above the chest with the elbows extended and forearms parallel to each other. Externally rotate the arms slightly so the elbows point away from the face (toward the knees).

▸ All repetitions begin from this position.

Starting positions

Downward and upward movements

Starting Position: Spotter

- Stand erect behind the head of the bench.
- Place the feet shoulder-width apart in a staggered stance with the knees slightly flexed.
- Grasp the bar with a closed, alternated grip.
- Hand the bar to the lifter.
- Guide the bar to a position over the lifter's chest.
- Release the bar smoothly.

Downward Movement: Lifter

- Begin the exercise by lowering the bar in an arc slowly and under control toward the nose, eyes, forehead, or the top of the head, depending on the length of the arms. Lifters with longer arms will lower the bar toward the top of the head and those with shorter arms will lower the bar toward the face.
- Keep the wrists stiff and the upper arms perpendicular to the floor and parallel to each other. No movement should occur at the shoulder joints; movement should occur only at the elbows.
- As the elbows begin to flex, they should point toward the knees (not out to the sides).
- Continue to lower the bar until it almost touches the head or face at its lowest position.
- Keep the head, torso, hips, and feet in a five-point body-contact position.

Downward Movement: Spotter

- Place the hands in a supinated grip position close to—but not touching—the bar as it descends.
- Slightly flex the knees, hips, and torso, and keep the back neutral when following the path of the bar.

Upward Movement: Lifter

- Push the bar upward under control by extending at the elbows back to the starting position. No movement should occur at the shoulder joints; movement should occur only at the elbows.
- Keep the upper arms and elbows stationary; they should not move forward or out as the bar rises.
- Maintain the same stationary five-point body-contact position; do not arch the low back, lift the head, raise the buttocks, or push up with the legs.
- Keep the wrists stiff and the upper arms perpendicular to the floor and parallel to each other.

▸ Continue to push the bar up until the elbows are fully extended but not forcefully locked.

▸ At the completion of the set, signal the spotter to take the bar, but keep a firm grip until the spotter gains full control of the bar.

Upward Movement: Spotter

▸ Keep the hands in a supinated grip position close to—but not touching—the bar as it ascends.

▸ Slightly extend the knees, hips, and torso, and keep the back neutral when following the path of the bar.

▸ At the lifter's signal after the set is completed, stand up and grasp the bar with a closed, alternated grip, take it from the lifter, and set it on the floor.

3.24 TRICEPS PUSHDOWN (MACHINE)

Video 3.24

Starting Position

- Stand under a high-pulley station with the torso erect, shoulders held back, back against the vertical back pad (if one is present), head in a neutral position, and eyes focused ahead.

- Grasp the bar evenly with a closed, pronated grip, approximately 6 to 12 inches (15 to 30 cm) wide (various bar attachments can be used for this exercise; the most common is an 18-inch [46 cm] straight bar).

- A minimum recommended grip width is close enough for the tips of the thumbs to touch each other when they are extended along the bar. A maximum distance is where the forearms are parallel to each other.

- Place the feet shoulder- or hip-width apart with the knees slightly flexed and the torso erect.

- Pull the bar down to position the upper arms and elbows against the sides of the torso with the forearms parallel to the floor (or slightly higher). Do not lean forward or turn the head to position an ear next to the cable; instead, keep the head in a neutral position with the cable directly in front of the nose. The body should be close enough to the machine so the cable hangs nearly perpendicular to the floor when the bar is grasped and held in the starting position.

- Hold the shoulders back, keep the upper arms and elbows pressed against the sides of the torso, and keep the abdominal muscles contracted. The selected load should be suspended above the remainder of the weight stack. All repetitions begin from this position.

Downward Movement

- Begin the exercise by pushing the bar down by extending at the elbows.

- Keep the wrists stiff and the upper arms perpendicular to the floor and pressed against the sides of the torso. No movement should occur at the shoulder joints; movement should occur only at the elbows.

- Continue to push the bar down until the elbows are fully extended but not forcefully locked.

- Maintain an erect torso and slightly flexed knee position; do not squat down slightly, lean forward, move the elbows backward, or move the cable to the right or left to help push the bar down.

Upward Movement

▸ Guide the bar slowly and under control back up to the starting position; do not allow the bar to jerk the arms upward.

▸ Keep the upper arms and elbows stationary; they should not move forward or out as the bar rises.

▸ Maintain the same stationary body position; do not move the head, torso, or feet as the bar rises.

▸ Keep the wrists stiff and the upper arms perpendicular to the floor and pressed against the sides of the torso.

▸ Continue to guide the bar up until the forearms are parallel to the floor (or slightly higher).

▸ At the completion of the set, slowly guide the bar under control to its resting position.

TRICEPS PUSHDOWN (MACHINE)

Starting position

Downward and upward movements

Forearm (Single-Joint) Exercises

Name	Description of the concentric action	PREDOMINANT MUSCLES INVOLVED	
		Muscle group or body area	Muscles
Wrist curl	Wrist flexion	Forearms	Flexor carpi radialis
			Flexor carpi ulnaris
			Palmaris longus
Wrist extension	Wrist extension	Forearms	Extensor carpi radialis brevis
			Extensor carpi radialis longus
			Extensor carpi ulnaris

Video 3.25

3.25   WRIST CURL

Starting Position

▸ Grasp the bar evenly with a closed, supinated grip about hip- to shoulder-width apart.

▸ Follow the preparatory body position and lifting guidelines to lift the bar off the floor to a position at the front of the thighs.

▸ Sit on one end of a flat bench and position the feet hip-width apart with the legs parallel to each other and the toes pointing straight ahead. Lean the torso forward to place the elbows and forearms on top of the thighs.

▸ Move the forearms forward until the wrists extend slightly beyond the patellae.

▸ Open the hands to allow the wrists to extend in order to rest the back of the hands on the patellae, and then roll the bar down so it is held by the fingertips. All repetitions begin from this position.

Upward Movement

▸ Begin the exercise by raising the bar by flexing the fingers and then the wrists.

Starting position

Upward and downward movements

UPPER BODY

▶ Keep the elbows and forearms stationary; do not jerk the shoulders backward or rise up on the toes to help raise the bar upward.

▶ Continue flexing the wrists as far as possible without lifting the wrists off the thighs.

Downward Movement

▶ Lower the bar slowly and under control to the starting position by extending the fingers and wrists; do not lift the elbows off the thighs.

▶ Maintain the same stationary body and arm positions with the feet flat on the floor.

▶ At the completion of the set, lift the arms off the thighs, slowly lean forward, and return the bar to the floor in a controlled manner.

3.26   WRIST EXTENSION

Video 3.26

Starting Position

▶ Grasp the bar evenly with a closed, pronated grip about hip- to shoulder-width apart.

▶ Follow the preparatory body position and lifting guidelines to lift the bar off the floor to a position at the front of the thighs.

▶ Sit on one end of a flat bench and position the feet hip-width apart with the legs parallel to each other and the toes pointing straight ahead. Lean the torso forward to place the elbows and forearms on the top of the thighs.

▶ Move the wrists forward until they are slightly beyond the patellae.

▶ Keep a closed grip on the bar but allow the wrists to flex toward the floor. All repetitions begin from this position.

Upward Movement

▶ Begin the exercise by raising the bar by extending the wrists.

▶ Keep the elbows and forearms stationary; do not jerk the shoulders backward or rise up on the toes to help raise the bar upward.

▶ Continue extending the wrists as far as possible without lifting the wrists off the thighs.

Starting position

Upward and downward movements

Downward Movement

- ► Lower the bar slowly and under control to the starting position; do not lift the elbows off the thighs.
- ► Maintain the same stationary body and arm positions with the feet flat on the floor.
- ► At the completion of the set, lift the arms off the thighs, slowly lean forward, and return the bar to the floor in a controlled manner.

CORE

PART IV

Core Exercises

Name	Description of the concentric action	PREDOMINANT MUSCLES INVOLVED	
		Muscle group or body area	Muscles
Bent-knee sit-up	Trunk flexion	Abdomen	Rectus abdominis
Abdominal crunch	Trunk flexion	Abdomen	Rectus abdominis
Front plank	Isometric	Abdomen	Rectus abdominis
			Transversus abdominis
			Obliques
		Low back	Erector spinae
Side plank	Isometric	Abdomen	Obliques
Stability ball rollout	Isometric	Abdomen	Rectus abdominis
			Iliopsoas
Stability ball pike	Hip flexion	Abdomen	Rectus abdominis
			Iliopsoas
Stability ball jackknife	Hip flexion	Abdomen	Rectus abdominis
			Iliopsoas
Abdominal crunch (machine)	Trunk flexion	Abdomen	Rectus abdominis
Stability ball abdominal crunch	Trunk flexion	Abdomen	Rectus abdominis
Stability ball reverse back extension	Trunk extension	Low back	Erector spinae

*Many core exercises involve more muscles than those listed here, and references vary in identifying which muscle or muscles are considered predominant.

CORE

4.1   BENT-KNEE SIT-UP

Video 4.1

Starting Position

- Lie in a supine position on a floor mat.
- Flex the knees to approximately 90 degrees and flex the hips to approximately 45 degrees to place the feet flat on the mat with the heels near the buttocks. The thighs, knees, and feet should be aligned with each other.
- Fold the arms across the chest or abdomen.
- All repetitions begin from this position.

Upward Movement

- Begin the exercise by flexing the neck to move the chin nearer to (but not touching) the upper chest and then curl the torso to lift the upper back off the mat.
- Maintain the same stationary lower body position with the arms folded across the chest; do not lift the feet off the mat as the upper body is raised.
- Continue to curl the torso toward the thighs until the upper back is off the mat.

Starting position

Upward and downward movements

Downward Movement

- Uncurl the torso, then extend the neck slowly and under control back to the starting position; do not lift the buttocks off the mat to help rebound for the next repetition.

- Maintain the same stationary lower body position and keep the arms folded across the chest.

4.2 ABDOMINAL CRUNCH

Video 4.2

Starting Position

- Lie in a supine position on a floor mat.
- Place the heels on a bench with the hips and knees flexed to approximately 90 degrees. The thighs, knees, and feet should be aligned with each other.
- Fold the arms across the chest or abdomen.
- All repetitions begin from this position.

Upward Movement

- Begin the exercise by flexing the neck to move the chin nearer to (but not touching) the upper chest and then curl the torso to lift the upper back off the mat.
- Maintain the same stationary lower body position with the arms folded across the chest; do not lift the feet off the bench as the upper body is raised.
- Continue to curl the torso toward the thighs until the upper back is off the mat.

Starting position   Upward and downward movements

Downward Movement

▶ Uncurl the torso, then extend the neck slowly and under control back to the starting position; do not lift the buttocks off the floor to help rebound for the next repetition or lift the feet from the bench.

▶ Maintain the same stationary lower body position and keep the arms folded across the chest.

4.3   FRONT PLANK

Video 4.3

Starting Position

▶ Kneel in a prone, quadruped position on the floor. The feet should be hip-width apart or slightly closer, with the foot, ankle, knee, and hip of each leg in a vertical plane. The palms of the hands should be flat on the floor approximately shoulder-width apart with the elbows pointing backward.

▶ Drop the elbows to the floor one at a time and position them directly under the shoulders with the forearms parallel to each other.

▶ Move the feet back one at a time to allow the hips and knees to extend so the abdomen and the front of the hips and legs rest on the floor.

Ending Position

▶ Elevate the hips so the ankles, knees, hips, shoulders, and head are in a straight line at a slight incline (the head end of the body will be higher than the feet end).

▶ Isometrically hold the torso in a rigid position with the hips posteriorly tilted to keep the lumbar spine in a neutral position.

▶ Keep the elbows directly under the shoulders.

▶ Maintain a neutral head position.

▶ At the end of the repetition, slowly lower the hips and legs to return to the starting position.

Starting position   Ending position

4.4   SIDE PLANK

Video 4.4

Starting Position

- Lie on the floor on the left side with the left elbow under the left shoulder.

- Position the left forearm perpendicular to the torso.

- Stack the right foot on top of the left foot with the right leg evenly on top of the left leg, or place the right foot on the floor immediately in front of the left foot. Stack the right arm evenly on top of the right side of the torso. The body's weight will be supported by the left arm.

Ending Position

- Use the outside of the left foot as the pivot, or anchor point, and elevate the hips so the left ankle, knee, hip, and shoulder are in a straight line. Keep the right foot and leg stacked on top of the left foot and leg—or alternatively, keep the right foot on the floor in front of the left foot—and the right arm stacked on top of the right side of the torso.

- Isometrically hold the torso in a rigid position.

- Keep the left elbow directly under the left shoulder.

- Keep the head in a neutral position with the eyes focused forward.

- At the end of the repetition, slowly lower the hips and legs to return to the starting position. Repeat the exercise for the right side.

Starting position   Ending position

CORE

4.5 STABILITY BALL ROLLOUT

Video 4.5

Starting Position

▶ Kneel facing the stability ball with the toes on the floor, upper body in an erect position, elbows extended, and hands touching the upper front side of the ball.

▶ While keeping the hands on the ball, reposition the knee and toe location to create a 90-degree angle at the knees and ankles with the knees, hips, and shoulders in a near-vertical plane.

Ending Position

▶ Keep the knees and toes on the floor; the elbows fully extended; the arms parallel to each other; and the knees, hips, and shoulders in a straight line. Extend the knees and flex the shoulders to roll the ball forward; keep the arms across the top of the ball until it comes close to the face.

▶ Isometrically hold the torso in a rigid position; do not let the hips sag toward the floor.

▶ At the end of the repetition, flex the knees and extend the shoulders to roll the arms back over the ball to return to the starting position.

Starting position

Ending position

4.6 STABILITY BALL PIKE

Video 4.6

Starting Position

- Kneel in front of a stability ball in a quadruped position with the body facing away from the ball, the hands underneath the shoulders approximately shoulder-width apart, and the knees underneath the hips approximately hip-width apart.

- Place the feet, one at a time, next to each other on top of the stability ball.

- While keeping the feet on the ball, extend the hips and knees and reposition the hands so that the body is in a prone plank position with the hands directly underneath the shoulders.

- Isometrically hold the torso in a rigid position with the elbows fully extended and the head in a neutral position. Maintain these positions during the exercise.

- All repetitions begin from this prone plank position.

Upward Movement

- While keeping the knees and elbows fully extended and the torso in a rigid position, begin the exercise by flexing the hips to roll the ball toward the chest until the toes are on top of the ball and the hips are directly over the shoulders.

- Keep the head in a neutral position during the upward movement.

CORE

Starting position   Upward and downward movements

Downward Movement

▶ Return to the starting position by allowing the hips to extend under control with the knees and elbows fully extended and the torso held rigid.

▶ Keep the head in a neutral position during the downward movement.

4.7 STABILITY BALL JACKKNIFE

Video 4.7

Starting Position

- Kneel in front of a stability ball in a quadruped position with the body facing away from the ball, the hands underneath the shoulders approximately shoulder-width apart, and the knees underneath the hips approximately hip-width apart.

- Place the feet, one at a time, next to each other on top of the stability ball.

- While keeping the feet on the ball, extend the hips and knees and reposition the hands so that the body is in a prone plank position with the hands directly underneath the shoulders.

- Isometrically hold the torso in a rigid position with the elbows fully extended and the head in a neutral position. Maintain these positions during the exercise.

- All repetitions begin from this prone plank position.

Forward Movement

- While keeping the knees and elbows fully extended and the torso in a rigid position, begin the exercise by raising the hips slightly and flexing the hips and knees to roll the ball toward the chest until the hips and knees are fully flexed.

- Keep the shoulders over the hands and the head in a neutral position.

Starting position   Forward and backward movements

CORE

CORE

Backward Movement

▸ Return to the starting position by allowing the hips and knees to extend under control with the elbows fully extended and the torso held rigid.

▸ Keep the shoulders over the hands and the head in a neutral position.

4.8 ABDOMINAL CRUNCH (MACHINE)

Video 4.8

Starting Position

- Sit in the machine with the feet on the floor and the legs behind the roller pads.
- The hips and knees should be flexed to approximately 90 degrees with the legs behind and in contact with the roller pads.
- Grasp the handles of the machine on each side of the head with the back of the upper arms pressed against the arm pads.
- All repetitions begin from this position.

Forward Movement

- Begin the exercise by flexing the torso to move the chest forward and down toward the thighs.
- Do not lift the hips or lower back from the pad.
- Continue to flex the torso until the elbows point toward the thighs.

Starting position

Forward and backward movements

Backward Movement

▶ Extend the torso slowly and under control back to the starting position.

▶ Do not lift or excessively extend the hips to help rebound for the next repetition.

▶ Maintain the same stationary lower body position with the hands grasping the handles of the machine.

4.9   STABILITY BALL ABDOMINAL CRUNCH

Video 4.9

Starting Position

- Sit on a stability ball with the feet flat on the floor.
- The hips and knees should be flexed to approximately 90 degrees. The thighs, knees, and feet should be aligned with each other.
- Walk the feet away from the ball until the mid to lower section of the back is in contact with the ball and the torso is approximately parallel to the floor.
- Fold the arms across the chest or hold them near the sides of the head.
- All repetitions begin from this position.

Upward Movement

- Begin the exercise by flexing the neck to move the chin nearer to (but not touching) the upper chest and then curl the torso to lift the upper back off the ball.
- Maintain the same stationary lower body position and keep the arms folded across the chest or near the sides of the head; do not lift the feet off the floor as the upper body is raised.
- Continue to curl the torso toward the thighs until the upper back is off the ball.

CORE

Starting position   Upward and downward movements

CORE

Downward Movement

▶ Uncurl the torso, then extend the neck slowly and under control back to the starting position; do not lift or excessively extend the hips to help rebound for the next repetition.

▶ Maintain the same stationary lower body position and keep the arms folded across the chest or near the sides of the head.

4.10 STABILITY BALL REVERSE BACK EXTENSION

Starting Position

- ▶ Kneel in front of and facing a stability ball.

- ▶ Roll forward onto the ball so that the abdomen rests on the top of the ball in a prone plank position, the torso is as parallel to the floor as body proportions allow, and the hands are positioned directly underneath or slightly in front of the shoulders on the floor.

- ▶ Hold the feet together throughout the exercise.

- ▶ Isometrically hold the torso in a rigid position with the elbows fully extended and the head in a neutral position. Maintain these positions during the exercise.

- ▶ All repetitions begin from this prone plank position.

Upward Movement

- ▶ Extend at the hips to bring the legs up in a straight line with the body.

- ▶ Keep the lower body in a rigid plank position with the spine held in a neutral position and the ankles in dorsiflexion. Do not rotate the hips during the movement.

Starting position   Upward and downward movements

Downward Movement

▸ Return to the starting position by allowing the hips to flex under control until the feet touch the floor.

▸ Keep the lower body in a rigid plank position with the spine held in a neutral position and the ankles in dorsiflexion.

ALTERNATIVE MODES AND NONTRADITIONAL IMPLEMENTS

PART V

Exercises Using Alternative Modes and Nontraditional Implements

Name	Description of the concentric action	PREDOMINANT MUSCLES INVOLVED	
		Muscle group or body area	Muscles
Two-arm kettlebell swing	Hip extension	Gluteals	Gluteus maximus
		Hamstrings	Semimembranosus
			Semitendinosus
			Biceps femoris
	Knee extension	Quadriceps	Vastus lateralis
			Vastus intermedius
			Vastus medialis
			Rectus femoris
Single-leg squat	Hip extension	Gluteals	Gluteus maximus
		Hamstrings	Semimembranosus
			Semitendinosus
			Biceps femoris
	Knee extension	Quadriceps	Vastus lateralis
			Vastus intermedius
			Vastus medialis
			Rectus femoris
Single-leg kettlebell Romanian deadlift	Hip extension	Gluteals	Gluteus maximus
		Hamstrings	Semimembranosus
			Semitendinosus
			Biceps femoris
Turkish get-up	Hip extension	Gluteals	Gluteus maximus
		Hamstrings	Semimembranosus
			Semitendinosus
			Biceps femoris
	Knee extension	Quadriceps	Vastus lateralis
			Vastus intermedius
			Vastus medialis
			Rectus femoris
	Trunk flexion	Abdomen	Rectus abdominis

(continued)

(continued)

Name	Description of the concentric action	PREDOMINANT MUSCLES INVOLVED	
		Muscle group or body area	**Muscles**
One-arm kettlebell clean	Hip extension	Gluteals	Gluteus maximus
		Hamstrings	Semimembranosus
			Semitendinosus
			Biceps femoris
	Knee extension	Quadriceps	Vastus lateralis
			Vastus intermedius
			Vastus medialis
			Rectus femoris
	Shoulder flexion	Deltoids	Anterior deltoid
	Elbow flexion	Biceps	Biceps brachii
One-arm kettlebell press	Shoulder flexion	Deltoids	Anterior deltoid
	Elbow extension	Triceps	Triceps brachii
Kettlebell front squat	Hip extension	Gluteals	Gluteus maximus
	Knee extension	Quadriceps	Vastus lateralis
			Vastus intermedius
			Vastus medialis
			Rectus femoris
Stability ball bridge to curl	Hip extension	Gluteals	Gluteus maximus
	Knee flexion	Hamstrings	Semimembranosus
			Semitendinosus
			Biceps femoris
Dumbbell renegade row	Shoulder flexion/ transverse adduction	Chest	Pectoralis major
		Shoulders	Anterior deltoid
	Scapular protraction (abduction)	Scapulae	Serratus anterior
		Chest	Pectoralis minor
	Elbow extension	Upper arm (posterior)	Triceps brachii
	Scapular retraction (adduction)	Upper back, midback	Middle trapezius
			Lower trapezius
			Rhomboids
	Shoulder extension	Back	Latissimus dorsi
			Teres major
		Shoulders	Posterior deltoid
	Elbow flexion	Upper arm (anterior)	Brachialis
			Biceps brachii
			Brachioradialis
	Isometric	Abdomen	Rectus abdominis
			Transversus abdominis
			Obliques
		Low back	Erector spinae

5.1   TWO-ARM KETTLEBELL SWING

Video 5.1

Starting Position

- Stand straddling a kettlebell with the feet flat between hip- and shoulder-width apart and the toes pointed straight ahead.

- Squat down with the hips lower than the shoulders and the elbows fully extended; grasp the kettlebell handle with both hands using a closed, pronated grip.

- Stand up to lift the kettlebell off the floor, then position the body with the back in a neutral spine position, the shoulders retracted and depressed, the heels in contact with the floor, and the eyes focused ahead (not seen in the photos). The hands are holding the kettlebell between the thighs with the elbows fully extended.

- While keeping the back in a neutral spine position, flex the hips and knees to approximately a quarter-squat position with the kettlebell hanging at arm's length between the thighs (not seen in the photos).

- All repetitions begin from this position.

Backward Movement

- Begin the exercise by flexing at the hips (with the knees held in the same starting position) and swinging the kettlebell between the legs.

- Keep the knees in a moderately flexed position with the back neutral and the elbows extended during the backward movement.

- Keep swinging the kettlebell between the legs until the torso is nearly parallel to the floor and the kettlebell is past the vertical line of the body.

Forward/Upward Movement

- When the backward swing reaches its end point, reverse the movement of the kettlebell by extending the hips and knees to move the kettlebell forward in an upward arc.

- Allow momentum to raise the kettlebell to approximately eye level. Keep the elbows extended and the back in a neutral spine position.

ALTERNATIVE

Downward/Backward Movement

- Allow the kettlebell to drop into the downswing; when the upper arms come into contact with the torso, flex the hips and knees to absorb the weight of the kettlebell.

- Keep the elbows fully extended and the back in a neutral position.

- Continue the downward-then-backward movement of the kettlebell by flexing the hips and knees until the kettlebell passes under and then behind the vertical line of the body.

- At the completion of the set, slow and then stop the momentum of the kettlebell and set it down on the floor.

TWO-ARM KETTLEBELL SWING

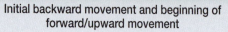

Starting position | Initial backward movement and beginning of forward/upward movement | End of forward/upward movement and beginning of downward/backward movement

5.2 SINGLE-LEG SQUAT

Starting Position

The initial position for this exercise—before one foot is placed on the bench or box—is identical to the initial position of the back squat exercise. If a bar is used, the bar is commonly placed *above* the posterior deltoids at the base of the neck in the high bar placement position. If dumbbells are used, they should be held at the sides of the torso with a closed, neutral grip. The photos for this exercise do not show a spotter, but if spotting is needed, two spotters should be used with one on each side of the bar.

- Stand in front of a bench or box that is approximately knee-height with the feet shoulder- to hip-width apart.

- Face away from the bench or box and place the instep of the right foot on top of the bench or box. Allow both knees to be slightly flexed with the torso in a nearly erect position and the shoulders held back, the head in a neutral position in relation to the spine, and the chest held up and out to create a neutral or slightly arched back.

- All repetitions begin from this position.

Downward Movement

- Flex the hip and knee of both legs simultaneously to lower the body in a vertical plane while keeping the torso-to-floor angle constant; do not round the upper back or lean forward as the bar is lowered.

- Keep the heel of the left foot flat on the floor and the instep of the right foot on top of the bench or box.

- Continue flexing the hips and knees until the left thigh is approximately parallel to the floor.

Upward Movement

- Raise the bar under control by actively extending the left hip and knee; focus on the left hip and knee, although the right hip and knee will passively extend as well.

- Maintain a position with a neutral spine and the torso upright.

▸ Extend the hips and knees at the same rate to keep the torso-to-floor angle constant. Do not allow the body's weight to shift forward onto the ball of the left foot.

▸ Keep the left knee aligned over the left foot; do not allow the knee to shift inward or outward as it extends.

▸ Continue focusing on extending the left hip and knee to return to the starting position.

▸ After completing a set with the left leg as the forward leg, repeat the procedure with the right leg as the forward leg.

SINGLE-LEG SQUAT

Starting position

Downward and upward movements

5.3 SINGLE-LEG KETTLEBELL ROMANIAN DEADLIFT

Video 5.3

This exercise can be performed with the kettlebell held in the hand of the same side of the body as the support leg (ipsilateral) or in the hand of the opposite side of the body as the support leg (contralateral). The text and the photos depict the contralateral single-leg kettlebell Romanian deadlift exercise.

Starting Position

- With the right hand, grasp a kettlebell with a closed, pronated grip.
- Stand on the left leg (as the support leg) with the hips and shoulders over the left foot and the body's weight on the left heel. The torso should be fully erect, with the shoulders held back, the head in a neutral position in relation to the spine, and the chest held up and out.
- Hold the kettlebell in front of the right thigh with the right elbow fully extended and the right foot slightly staggered back.
- All repetitions begin from this position.

Downward Movement

- Allow the left support knee to slightly flex, and then rigidly hold that position throughout the movement.
- Begin the exercise by allowing the torso to flex forward at the hip of the left support leg.
- Keep the right shoulder, hip, knee, and ankle aligned as the torso flexes forward; the movement takes place only at the hip of the left support leg. Do not rotate the hips as the kettlebell is lowered.
- Keep the knee of the left support leg in a slightly flexed position with the shoulders held in the same retracted position.
- Keep the back neutral with the head in a neutral position and the right elbow still fully extended.
- Lower the kettlebell until the torso and the right leg are approximately parallel to the floor.

Upward Movement

▸ Extend the hip of the left support leg to return to the starting position.

▸ Keep the knee of the left support leg in a slightly flexed position and the back neutral during the upward movement.

▸ Do not hyperextend the torso or neck, or flex the right elbow.

▸ After completing a set with the left leg as the support leg and the kettlebell held in the right hand, repeat the exercise with the right leg as the support leg and the kettlebell held in the left hand.

SINGLE-LEG KETTLEBELL ROMANIAN DEADLIFT

Starting position

Downward and upward movements

5.4   TURKISH GET-UP

Video 5.4

Starting Position

- Begin the exercise by lying on the floor in a supine position with a kettlebell near the left shoulder (not seen in the photos).

- Slightly turn toward the kettlebell and grasp it with the left hand in a closed, pronated grip (not seen in the photos). Use the right hand to help lift the kettlebell. The bell of the kettlebell should be positioned against the back of the hand and wrist.

- Flex the left hip and knee to approximately a 45-degree angle with the left foot flat on the floor.

- Position the right leg flat on the floor with the right ankle dorsiflexed to point the toes up.

- Lift the kettlebell over the face with both arms and then remove the right hand. The grip of the kettlebell in the left hand should remain near the corner of the handle and near the thumb on the palm of the hand.

- Keep the left elbow fully extended with the left arm pointing toward the ceiling during the exercise to hold the kettlebell over the left shoulder.

- Position the right arm flat on the floor at approximately a 45-degree angle away from the right side of the body with the elbow fully extended.

- All repetitions begin from this position.

Upward Movement

- While keeping the eyes focused on the kettlebell, begin the exercise by pushing up against the kettlebell. To do so, simultaneously push into the floor with the left foot to rotate the hips and torso so that the body is balanced on the right forearm and right hip (To the elbow). Keep the right leg, right ankle, left knee, and left foot in the same starting position.

- Continue to press up against the kettlebell and transition from the right forearm to the right hand (To the hand).

- With the left foot still flat on the floor, extend the left hip until the left knee is in approximately a 90-degree flexed position. The three points of contact on the floor should be both feet and the right hand (High post). The arms will be in a straight line nearly perpendicular to the floor with the kettlebell directly above both shoulders, elbows, and the right hand. Keep the eyes focused on the kettlebell.

ALTERNATIVE

▶ While holding the left hip and knee in the same position, sweep the right leg underneath and behind the body to place the right knee and foot on the floor behind the hips (Sweep the leg).

▶ Extend the right hip while pressing up against the kettlebell to lift the right hand off the floor and bring the torso to a fully upright position (Up tall). The lower body will be in a lunge position with the right knee directly underneath the right hip and shoulder, and the left hip and knee at approximately 90-degree angles.

▶ Shift the body's weight to the left leg and push up against the kettlebell; push down toward the floor with the left foot while fully extending the left hip and knee (not seen in the photos).

▶ Complete the upward movement by stepping forward with the right foot to place it next to the left foot with the kettlebell held directly over the left shoulder (Stand up).

TURKISH GET-UP

Starting position   To the elbow   To the hand

Downward Movement

▶ Begin the downward movement by pressing up against the kettlebell and extending the right leg straight back into a lunge position.

▶ Drop the right knee straight down to the floor. The right shoulder, hip, and knee should be in the same vertical plane.

▶ While continuing to press up against the kettlebell, focus the eyes on the kettlebell and bring the right hand to the floor. The arms will create a line that is close to perpendicular to the floor.

▶ Keeping the eyes focused on the kettlebell, extend the left hip, and sweep the right leg underneath the hips and then in front of the body with the left foot remaining flat on the floor and the left knee flexed to approximately 90 degrees. Be sure the left hip is fully extended and aligned with the shoulder and knee and that the right knee is extended and the ankle is dorsiflexed.

ALTERNATIVE

High post   Sweep the leg   Up tall

▶ Flex the left hip to drop the body down to sit on the floor. Keep the eyes focused on the kettlebell. The left knee should be flexed to approximately 45 degrees, with the right elbow fully extended and the right hand on the floor.

▶ Continue to press up against the kettlebell with the left arm fully extended, and lower the right elbow to the floor to support the body's weight.

▶ Slowly lower the body to the starting position.

▶ After completing a set with the kettlebell in the left hand, repeat the exercise with the kettlebell in the right hand and the right foot flat on the floor.

TURKISH GET-UP

Stand up

5.5 ONE-ARM KETTLEBELL CLEAN

Video 5.5

Starting Position

- Stand straddling a kettlebell with feet flat between hip- and shoulder-width apart and the toes pointed straight ahead.

- Squat down with the hips lower than the shoulders and the right elbow fully extended; grasp the kettlebell handle with the right hand using a closed, pronated grip.

- Stand up to lift the kettlebell off the floor, then position the body with the back neutral, the shoulders retracted and depressed, the heels in contact with the floor, and the eyes focused ahead. The right hand holds the kettlebell in front of the right thigh with the elbow fully extended.

- While keeping the back neutral, flex the hips and knees to approximately a quarter-squat position with the kettlebell hanging at arm's length between the thighs (not seen in the photos).

- All repetitions begin from this position.

Backward Movement

- Begin the exercise by flexing the torso farther forward at the hips (with the knees held in the same starting position) and swinging the kettlebell between the legs.

- Keep the knees in a moderately flexed position with the back neutral and the right elbow extended during the backward movement.

- Keep swinging the kettlebell between the legs until the torso is nearly parallel to the floor and the kettlebell is past the vertical line of the body.

Forward/Upward Movement

- When the backward swing reaches its end point, reverse the movement of the kettlebell by extending the hips and knees to move the kettlebell forward.

ALTERNATIVE

ALTERNATIVE

- Rather than allowing momentum to raise the kettlebell in an upward arc to approximately eye level with the elbows extended and the arms moving away from the torso (as in the two-arm kettlebell swing), allow momentum to raise the kettlebell while keeping the right upper arm in contact with the body.

- When the kettlebell reaches the position where the right upper arm would move away from the torso, quickly shrug the right shoulder and then flex the right elbow to pull the kettlebell back and up (not in an arc) in front of the torso; this is the transition.

Catch

- As the kettlebell reaches it maximum height, loosen the grip and quickly rotate the right arm under the kettlebell.

- Catch the kettlebell in a racked position with the right upper arm next to the torso; the right elbow pointing toward the floor; and the kettlebell against the back of the right hand, wrist, or forearm (depending on the size of the kettlebell and length of the arm).

ONE-ARM KETTLEBELL CLEAN

| On ground (grasping the kettlebell) | Starting position (standing) | Swing between legs |

To begin the next repetition, unrack the kettlebell from the right shoulder, uncurl the right arm at the elbow, lower the kettlebell to arm's length between the thighs, and allow the momentum of the kettlebell to drop it into the downswing between the legs. Flex the hips and knees to absorb the weight of the kettlebell and then follow the guidelines for the backward movement. After completing a set with the right hand holding the kettlebell, repeat the exercise with the left hand holding the kettlebell.

Transition   Catch

5.6 ONE-ARM KETTLEBELL PRESS

Video 5.6

Starting Position

▶ Follow the starting position, backward movement, and forward/upward movement guidelines of the one-arm kettlebell clean exercise to get in the correct starting position for this exercise. (Note that although the photos for this exercise show the kettlebell held in the left hand and those for the one-arm kettlebell clean exercise show the kettlebell held in the right hand, the same overall technique guidelines apply to both exercises.)

▶ All repetitions begin from this position.

Upward Movement

▶ Begin the exercise by flexing the left shoulder and extending the left elbow to press the kettlebell overhead. The right arm remains at the right side of the body.

Starting position

Upward and downward movements

- As the kettlebell is pressed overhead, externally rotate the left shoulder so that the left wrist and forearm move from a neutral position to a pronated position with the left elbow fully extended.
- Keep the spine neutral and the eyes looking forward. Do not allow the spine to flex laterally during the upward movement.

Downward Movement

- Allow the kettlebell to lower slowly and under control back to the starting position; do not flex the torso forward as the kettlebell is lowered.
- As the kettlebell is lowered, internally rotate the left shoulder so that the left wrist and forearm move back to the starting, neutral position.
- After completing a set with the left hand holding the kettlebell, repeat the exercise with the right hand holding the kettlebell.

5.7   KETTLEBELL FRONT SQUAT

Video 5.7

Starting Position

- Stand straddling a kettlebell with the feet flat and hip- to shoulder-width apart and the toes pointed straight ahead.

- Squat down with the hips lower than the shoulders and the elbows fully extended (not seen in the photos); grasp the kettlebell on both sides of the handle with a closed, neutral grip.

- Return to a standing position with the kettlebell held near the chest, the back in a neutral spine position, the shoulders retracted and depressed, the heels in contact with the floor, and the eyes focused ahead.

- All repetitions begin from this position.

Downward Movement

- Begin the downward movement by flexing the hips and knees slowly and under control.

Starting position   Downward and upward movements

- Maintain a neutral or slightly arched back and keep the kettlebell close to the body; do not allow the heels to rise off the floor during the downward movement.

- Keep the knees aligned over the feet; do not allow the knees to shift inward or outward as they flex.

- Continue the downward movement until one of these three events occurs (they determine the maximum range of motion, or the lowest squat position):

  1. The thighs are parallel to the floor (if achievable).
  2. The torso begins to round or flex forward.
  3. The heels rise off the floor.

- Actual squat depth is dependent on lower body joint flexibility.

- Keep the body tight and under control; do not bounce or relax the legs or torso at the bottom of the movement.

Upward Movement

- Stand up under control by extending the hips and knees.

- Maintain a neutral or slightly arched back and keep the kettlebell close to the body. Resist the tendency to lean forward by keeping the head tilted slightly back and holding the chest up and out.

- Continue pushing up with the body's weight evenly distributed between the heel and midfoot of both feet to keep them in contact with the floor and the hips under the body's center of mass. Do not allow the body's weight to shift forward onto the balls of the feet.

- Keep the knees aligned over the feet; do not allow the knees to shift inward or outward as they extend.

- Continue the upward movement at an even rate until the hips and knees are fully extended to return to the starting position.

ALTERNATIVE

5.8 STABILITY BALL BRIDGE TO CURL

Video 5.8

Starting Position

- Lie supine on the floor with a stability ball near the feet.
- Place the heels and calves on the upper front side of the ball with the ankles dorsiflexed. The knees should be fully extended with the head, back, and buttocks flat on the floor.
- Position the arms on the floor perpendicular to the torso with the elbows fully extended.
- All repetitions begin from this position.

Upward Movement

- Begin the exercise by extending the hips so that the body is in a straight line from the shoulders to the ankles (Bridge). Then flex the knees to roll the ball toward the body and bring the heels in toward the buttocks (Curl).
- Keep the hips rigid throughout the movement; do not let them sag toward the floor.

Starting position

Bridge

- Keep the head and arms in the same starting position and the legs parallel to each other.
- Continue bringing the heels toward the buttocks until the knees are flexed to approximately 90 degrees.

Downward Movement

- Return to the starting position by extending the knees under control.
- Keep the head neutral and in contact with the floor.
- Keep the arms on the floor perpendicular to the torso with the elbows fully extended.

Curl

5.9   DUMBBELL RENEGADE ROW

Video 5.9

Starting Position

▶ Assume the top push-up position with the elbows fully extended; hold a dumbbell in each hand approximately shoulder-width apart using a closed, neutral grip. Keep the head, neck, shoulders, spine, hips, thighs, knees, lower legs, and ankles aligned.

▶ Keep the feet hip- to shoulder-width apart to maintain balance throughout the movement.

▶ All repetitions begin from this position.

Downward Movement

▶ Begin the exercise by allowing the shoulders to extend and the elbows to flex to lower the body toward the floor.

▶ Maintain a neutral head position and isometrically hold the torso in a rigid position.

▶ Continue lowering the body until it is close to the floor.

Starting position   Downward movement

Upward Movements

- Flex the shoulders and extend the elbows to push the body back up to the starting position.

- Maintain a neutral head position and isometrically hold the torso in a rigid position.

- After reaching the starting position, isometrically contract the core muscles and the muscles of the left shoulder, then retract the right scapula, extend the right shoulder, and flex the right elbow to pull the right dumbbell up alongside the right side of the body.

- After the dumbbell is alongside the body, pause and then lower the dumbbell back to the floor. Maintain the head, torso, and lower body positions, and repeat the rowing motion with the left arm (not seen in the photos); this sequence is one repetition.

Upward movements

About the NSCA

The **National Strength and Conditioning Association** (NSCA) is the world's leading organization in the field of sport conditioning. Drawing on the resources and expertise of the most recognized professionals in strength and conditioning, sport science, performance research, education, and sports medicine, the NSCA is the world's trusted source of knowledge and training guidelines for coaches and athletes. The NSCA provides the crucial link between the lab and the field.